W9-AJO-784

A Dozen Ways to Sunday

ALSO BY MONTEL WILLIAMS

BodyChange™
(co-authored with Wini Linguvic)

Life Lessons and Reflections

Mountain, Get out of My Way!

Practical Parenting
(co-authored with Jeffrey Gardère, Ph.D.)

❃ ❃ ❃

A Dozen Ways to Sunday

Stories of Hope and Courage

Montel Williams

with Daniel Paisner

MOUNTAIN
MOVERS
PRESS

an imprint of
Hay House, Inc.
Carlsbad, California • Sydney, Australia

Copyright © 2001 by Montel Williams

Published and distributed in the United States by:
Mountain Movers Press, an imprint of Hay House, Inc.,
P.O. Box 5100, Carlsbad, CA 92018-5100
(800) 654-5126 • (800) 650-5115 (fax) • www.hayhouse.com

Editorial supervision: Jill Kramer • *Design:* Charles McStravick
Photography: Jay Lee (except for high school photo at
bottom of pg. 76, and photo of Bald Eagles at top of pg. 36)

CIP data available from the Library of Congress.

ISBN 1-58825-005-9

04 03 02 01   5 4 3 2
1st printing, October 2001
2nd printing, October 2001

Printed in the United States of America

*To everyone who has ever stepped outside
of themselves to help another.
You make the world a
better place for us all.*

CONTENTS

Acknowledgments

I'd like to thank Alyson Colingo for her passionate vision beneath the surface of the lives *she* touched—and who touched *her*—while compiling these stories; Jay Lee for shuttering the soul of each image captured; and Daniel Paisner for once again helping me bring my words to life.

And most important, I'd like to thank my kids Ashley, Maressa, Montel II, and Wynter Grace. They are my rocks and help me keep my hope and courage.

INTRODUCTION

Ten years ago, when I first started hosting my talk show, *Montel*, I was not prepared for the unshakable impressions that would be left on me by the parade of fascinating individuals who march before me every day. I'm telling you, not a day goes by that I don't scratch my head and think, *Man, I've seen it all.* Every kind of raw, basic emotion. Every conceivable family dynamic. Every possible triumph over every impossible adversity. Every good turn done for no reason other than that it was the right thing to do. I've seen every way that someone can be surprised, inspired, and otherwise moved by the actions of another person, and it stretches from my very first season on the air to the most recent. So, I've seen it all. And then some.

This book is about the "and then some." It's a chance for me to shine a light on some of the ennobling ways in which some people out there are living their lives: People who have been dealt a lousy hand that they've managed to play in a winning way. People who have found places in their hearts for the outcast and downtrodden. People who have counted their blessings and come up with some to spare. People who have made a life out of no life at all.

It always strikes me as a powerful thing—the ways in which we human beings can surprise each other, the ways in which we can surprise ourselves.

You know, as I worked to compile the profiles you're about to read, I couldn't help but think how my own life must look from outside my own skin. In some ways, these past couple of years, I've been living with some of the same uncertainties, some of the same imbalances, and some of the same hurdles that are facing the good people here. The same, but different, which is always the case, isn't it? We're all basically the same at the bottom, but up top, we're all kinds of different.

With me, the similarities have to do with facing down the hard times and daring the good times to come looking for me. If you've watched my show with any regularity over the past few seasons, you'll know that my life hasn't been smooth. I've been diagnosed with multiple sclerosis (MS). My marriage has ended. My days are now filled with thoughts of finding a cure, beating back a crippling disease, and finding some kind of toehold for the rest of my life. I'm constantly wrestling with some big-time issues, yet I press on—which is essentially what we all do, in our own private ways, each and every day we walk this planet. We do the best we can. We reach out to others. We move forward.

What it comes down to, I think, is faith. For a lot of people, myself included, that gets defined as faith in God, in a purpose that extends beyond our time on this earth. For others, and I include myself in this mix as well, that faith lies in ourselves, in our own strength, resolve, and vision. Let's face it, there are as many paths to faith as there are individuals to travel those paths, and one of the goals of this book is to highlight just a few of the compelling ways in which people have answered their own call. That's how we got to the title *A Dozen Ways to Sunday*, but why stop at a dozen? Underneath these dozen profiles, there are a dozen more. And a dozen more beyond that. And so on.

Let me make an important point: All of my royalties from this book have been earmarked for the foundation I've set up for MS research, because I'm just as doggedly determined as the people you're going to read about here. Doctors tell me that there's no known cure for what I've got, and I refuse to accept it. We live in the kind of wondrous times where *anything* is possible, so don't tell me this one's out of our reach. Multiple sclerosis, spinal cord injuries, cancer, Parkinson's, Alzheimer's . . . there are cures to be found. All we need, on the societal level, is the time and money and willpower to go looking.

Money and willpower I've got, and those will be my never-ending contributions to the cause. It's the time I'm not so sure about. That's the one thing that gets to me since my diagnosis—the way there's now a clock on my rear. I can be feeling fine and strong for a stretch, but I know that that stretch won't last indefinitely. I know that there will be bad stretches mixed in with the good. I can be enjoying a great vacation with my kids, or spending time with them at Christmas, but I know that those days might run out on me eventually. It's the way everything now has to be measured that gets me reeling. That's what nobody talks about: Before the disease itself can cripple you, the thought of what's to come and what might never come around again just knocks the wind right out of you. But we *will* find a cure. Count on it. For what ails me, and for what ails us all. In time. It might not be in *my* time, and I'll just have to deal with that, but it will be in *our* time. And it will be soon.

Now it won't be because of the money any single person is able to raise and contribute to research, or the advances or ingenuity of any single scientist. It will be because of the collective will and positive energy flowing from all of us who set our minds on the right prize. Like the people who are profiled in this book: The empty-nest couple from Arizona who found it in their hearts (and in their retirement budget!) to adopt ten siblings. The fifth-grade students from California who shaved their heads so their classmate wouldn't feel ostracized when he lost his hair in chemotherapy. The resourceful woman from Pennsylvania who spearheaded a nationwide effort to provide more than 100,000 blankets and sleeping bags for the homeless, all homemade from recycled or donated materials. The Holocaust survivor from the former Czechoslovakia (by way of Long Island) who has made it his calling to enlighten young people on the dangers of prejudice and hatred. The ex-con from Brooklyn whose late-in-life love affair with animals has left him no choice but to fight for the rights and safekeeping of every stray dog and cat in his path, and every other animal besides. The allergist from Arkansas who wanted to provide a summer-camp experience for his patients with asthma, and wound up launching a nonprofit summer program with specific weekly sessions for kids with asthma, arthritis, cancer, epilepsy, cerebral palsy, spina bifida, and muscular dystrophy—all staffed by volunteer physicians, nurses, and experts in each field.

Some of these folks have already been profiled on *Montel*, my talk show. Others will be in the future. Happily, there wouldn't be enough segments in a thousand television seasons to air every worthwhile story unfolding in our neighborhoods, which takes me to the underlying purpose of this effort: I'm not out to merely celebrate *these* good people, but everyone like them. I'm not out to merely raise money for MS research, but to raise our collective conscience, to drive home the message that all of us are players in this great, unwieldy, unpredictable drama called life. Yes, most definitely, we've all got a role, and good things can't help but happen when we rise to meet that role with a selfless outlook and boundless good cheer.

There's a clock on all of us, is what it comes down to. There's no such thing "as all the time in the world." But what we can learn from these stirring individuals, and what I've learned from the hand I've been dealt, is that there is all the time we need. To give something back. To push a thing forward. To press on.

Together, my friends, we can move mountains, and here are just a few ways to start with the pushing. . . .

❀ ❀ ❀

The Hughes family at home
in Mesa, Arizona.

CHAPTER ONE

All in the Family

*T*he first time I heard about the Hughes family of Mesa, Arizona, I thought maybe I didn't hear it right. The word that got to my producers and me was that Shirley and Van Hughes, a couple of empty-nesters and the grandparents of two, had opened their hearts and their home to ten brothers and sisters in the largest-ever sibling adoption in U.S. history. Ten kids, ranging in age from about 3 to 15, all from the same mother, all bouncing around in the "system" after being discovered by authorities in the kind of squalor that makes headlines.

I thought that this mass adoption was one of the top ten most selfless things I'd ever heard, so we dug in to learn more. What came back in the digging was that Shirley and Van were even more giving than any of us had thought, and their new brood was even more of a handful than any of us had imagined, which in itself was a tribute to these two generous souls.

As with almost every remarkable turn of events, this one didn't just happen. For a long time, back when their two biological sons, Jason and Jeff, were still in the house, Shirley and Van used to kick around the notion of foster parenting. It was pie-in-the-sky kind of talk, something to think about when the boys were grown, a place to put their boundless love when their own children didn't need a daily dose of the stuff. They didn't know anybody who was involved in foster care, but they'd read about it, seen stories about it on TV, had done some research, and thought that maybe it would be a good fit somewhere down the road. At the time, though, things were busy enough. Van was a career Navy man (he was in the military police), and Shirley held a job in electronics. Soon enough, their boys were married, with kids of their own, and the whole bunch of them were still living under the same roof, so the idea of taking care of someone else's kids was pushed to the back of their thinking.

But then, something happened: Jason and Jeff moved out with their young families into their own homes just a few miles away, and Shirley and Van found themselves with a whole lot of time, space, and devotion on their hands. It was 1994, and Van was working as a chief petty officer at the Naval Training Center in San Diego, and when he came home to Mesa on the weekends, same as he always did, he found the house way too quiet for his liking.

"There was one night," he recalls, "maybe two or three months after the boys had left, when

I went to shut our bedroom door, because, you know, we always shut our bedroom door. Our daughters-in-law had been living there with our two grandkids. There was always something going on, and we tried to respect each other's privacy. So I'm about to shut the door and Shirley says to me, 'What are you doing shutting the door?' I thought about it for a bit and said, 'Well, I'm in my underwear.' And then she thought about this for a bit, until she finally said, 'But Van, there's nobody here.'"

"I couldn't get over it," Shirley recalls, cleaning up the details of her husband's story so that it comes out just right. "The kids were gone, and he was still closing the door like we had a full house."

Van couldn't sleep that night, just as he hadn't been able to sleep all that well since he and Shirley had the place to themselves. He caught himself thinking, *I can't stand it; it's really too quiet here,* and he realized that it was the constant quiet that was keeping him up nights. Then he reached out to his wife to see if she was still awake. She was. "You remember what we talked about," he asked her, "six, seven years ago, seeing about some kind of foster-care program?"

"I remember," she said.

"Well, do you still want to do that?" he asked. "'Cause I do."

Shirley had been thinking pretty much the same thing, and the next morning she was into the Yellow Pages, looking for the right listing. Before the week was out, they had a meeting set up with a local branch of Child Protective Services (CPS). In Arizona, couples looking to become foster parents had to take a seven-week course before CPS or the Department of Economic Security (DES) would place a child in their care, and Shirley and Van signed on with the same kind of enthusiasm prospective parents might bring to a birthing class. They soaked up all they could about caring for handicapped, abused, and/or neglected children. They learned how to help a child compensate for various learning disabilities. They let themselves be walked through every kind of sensitive scenario, became familiar with the family court system, and came to understand what it was like to be a child bounced from one foster home to another, one agency to another, from one ray of hope to the next. They decided early on that they would like to care for a sibling group of some kind, based on the thinking that it was hard enough to be placed into foster care without also being split from a brother or sister, and they put this down on their application.

"The one thing we insisted on," Van explains, "was that the kids be on the young side. Three, five, seven years old, somewhere in there. We weren't ready for teenagers, not at that point. All we knew, going in, was that we'd heard a lot of tales of foster parents getting killed by foster children. Killed, beaten, robbed . . . all kinds of things. We were a little scared at first, and thought maybe if we got to these kids early, we'd have a shot at turning their lives around, making a real difference. We thought if we got them small enough, there was no problem we couldn't handle."

Just a couple weeks later, in March of 1995, Shauna and Michael, ages five and two, arrived. The DES report said their mother was a drug addict, unable to care for the children herself, and their father had not been identified. The kids were as cute as could be, and in tremendous need, but they had some serious emotional problems. It was just like some of the situations Shirley and Van had learned about in class, only here it was in their home, for real. And despite the "small" package, there were some big issues for Shirley and Van to contend with. The children had been abused, and this played out in a variety of troubling ways. Michael, even at two, would bite and kick and hit; Shirley and Van had to approach him cautiously to calm him down so they wouldn't get hurt themselves. Shauna was prone to having temper tantrums and uncontrollable fits of screaming. There was simply no quieting this child. At one point, Van thought he'd found a way to "fix her clock," as he says, and he lay down on the kitchen floor, where Shauna lay hollering her pretty little head off, and started hollering himself. Kicking and screaming, the whole deal. But Shauna just looked at him like he was plain crazy and started screaming even louder.

Shirley looked on and felt powerless to do anything to gain control of the situation. She thought, *Dear God, just tell me what to do with this child.* She really prayed about it. It was that, or throw up her hands in despair. Just then, she thought about singing. In the middle of all of this kicking and hollering, she launched into one of her favorite Christian songs, in full voice:

Our God, is an awesome God.
He reigns, from Heaven above . . .

The louder she sang, the louder Shauna screamed, but Shirley kept at it, until finally Shauna started singing with her. The little girl knew the song from church, and they sang it all the way through together, and there was one problem solved, for the time being.

Gradually, Shirley and Van got a handle on how to deal with these two children, and they helped build a bridge of respect and trust that stands to this day. They also learned what it was like to be a part of the state's foster-care system— monthly visits from a licensing worker and from the DES, periodic attorney visits, monthly staffing meetings, and in some cases, a monthly visit from a Court Appointed Special Advocate (CASA) worker. All kinds of new people, in and out of their home, on a constant basis, to the point where they sometimes felt that their lives were no longer their own.

Indeed, they weren't, and that was just fine with these good people. All it took was one smile from little Michael, one positive interaction with Shauna, one hug they weren't expecting, and Shirley and Van would feel that they'd made a good bargain. Their own boys, too, fell into their parents' new role with pride and enthusiasm. Their grandson, Andrew, matched up in age with Michael, so the little boy had a constant playmate, and before long, Shirley and Van started thinking of adding another little girl to the mix, for Shauna's sake. Before they could talk each other out of the idea, Shirley was on the phone trying to arrange a new placement, which would put her at the state-mandated limit for foster children under her care. See, even though she and Van were very much together in their marriage, the court looked upon Van's out-of-state military assignment as a separation and regarded Shirley as a single parent. A married couple, living together, could take in as many as five foster children; a single parent could only take in three.

While they waited for a little girl to round out their picture, Shirley and Van assessed their new situation. Money was tight, but the budget was manageable. Van had grown up poor, and he knew what that was like. The state offered a stipend of about $11 per day, per foster child, but that didn't go very far once you factored in all the start-up costs associated with foster care. Shauna and Michael had come to them with nothing—a couple of plastic bags, packed like trash, with old, ratty clothes Shirley couldn't see keeping—so they each had to be outfitted from scratch. They needed bedding, furniture, toys, and books. Plus, the house had to be brought into compliance with child-safety codes. Locks had to be refitted, wall sockets covered, and loose wires and cords concealed. The Hugheses had an above-ground pool out back, and there were all kinds of overhauls they had to make to the fencing and landscaping to bring the thing up to code. They were forever playing catch-up, laying out monies, waiting for the end-of-the-month check from the state to reimburse some of their costs. "It really is a major commitment," Van says, of the financial obligations that go along with foster care. "You'd think that it's enough of an emotional commitment and a lifestyle commitment as it is, but they pile on all this red tape on top of that, and then there are all these expenses. Somebody needs to do something about it to make it easier."

Three-year-old Maria arrived in June of 1995, and Shirley and Van were delighted by the additional burden. Unlike Shauna and Michael, this child was as quiet as a still-life—so quiet, in fact, that there were times they almost forgot she was there. And she was dutiful, too. You'd tell her to sit quietly on the couch, and off she'd go to sit quietly on the couch, indefinitely, until you told her otherwise. It was almost funny. She was incredibly shy. Shirley and Van couldn't get her to string two words together. Now, of course, she's a regular chatterbox, but in the beginning, she was fairly withdrawn.

Maria's CASA worker, a woman named Jean Peirce, reported that the child had two brothers the state was still trying to place, and they wondered if Shirley or Van knew anybody who might be interested in taking them in. It was, Shirley knew, a loaded question. Jean Peirce was fully aware that the Hughes's situation meant that they could only care for three foster children at one time, but she also knew their hearts could accommodate a couple more. So, she put it out there for Shirley to consider.

And so Shirley did some considering. She considered how attached she'd become in such a short time to Shauna and Michael. She considered the quick bond she was forming with little Maria—the shy, whip-smart girl who came a little bit further out of her shell each day. She considered the ways she and Van were helping to turn these young lives around, and the ways they might turn around two more. And she considered the triple-shot of energy that fueled her household now that these three kids were in their care and in their midst.

She called Van at the base in San Diego to let him in on her thinking. She thought that maybe he could seek an early out from the Navy, take some sort of civilian job back in Arizona, so they could qualify to care for Maria's two brothers. It didn't seem to Shirley that she was asking all that much—surely, no more than Van would have thought to do himself once he knew the full story—so all she was really doing was bringing him up to speed. Still, Van was taken aback by her suggestion. He thought, *Whoa! This is something we need to talk through when I get home this weekend. This isn't a conversation for the telephone. This is a big decision.*

That next weekend home, Shirley and Van talked, only there wasn't much to say. These kids needed them. Maria needed to be with her brothers. Van had 18 years in the Navy at this point, on a good career track, just two years shy of a full pension, but there was no real dilemma once he knew the situation. "To tell you the truth, I never even looked at what I'd miss," he says now. "I really didn't care. It's a hard choice to make, I'm not denying it, but when you break it down, you see it clear. When you leave this earth, what have you done with your life if you just log your 20 years in the Navy, take your pension, and die? Put that up against helping to keep a family together, and it doesn't even come close. It was a good thing to do."

It took some maneuvering to get Van his "early out" from the Navy, including a phone call to the Pentagon, during which time Shirley was doing some maneuvering of her own to bring Juan, 6, and Jose, 5, into the family. The boys, like their little sister, had been abused and neglected, and they carried the scars of their hard young lives. Jose, in particular, was incredibly angry—at everybody, and everything—but by now, Shirley was a practiced hand at leading her young charges down a steady, sure path. She found that she had an easy way with children, an innate ability to talk to them, a willingness to listen. She respected them, and they appeared to thrive in that respect—even a kid like Juan, who continued to lash out, but a little less violently each day. His soft spots became easier and easier to find.

Not long after Juan and Jose joined the family, a DES worker called with the news that a man had come forward claiming to be Shauna and Michael's father. He agreed to a DNA test to establish paternity, and when the results proved that he was their father, he petitioned for custody. Shirley and Van were happy for the children, even though they mourned their departure. Their leaving coincided with a request from CASA worker Jean Peirce to help organize a family reunion for Maria, Juan, and Jose and their seven siblings. Understand, these were siblings that Shirley and Van didn't know anything about until the idea of the get-together surfaced. The three kids they had living with them had never talked about any brothers or sisters, and Shirley and Van flashed each other a knowing glance that seemed to say, *Look at the hoops we jumped through just to keep these three together! And now we find out there are seven more!*

The story, as Shirley and Van were now discovering, was that their three foster kids were in fact fathered by the same man, but their mother had seven other kids with three (or, possibly, four) other men. It was a strange mix. The oldest four shared the same father; the next in line had a different father; the next three (Juan, Jose, and Maria) had the same father; and the two youngest had either the same or two different fathers. All of the girls (and there were four of them) carried their mother's last name, Baumea. Some of the boys bore their fathers' names, and some their mothers', depending on whether the father was with them at the time of birth. They were mostly Hispanic, like their mother, with some of her American Indian blood, mixed with the variously Hispanic and Native American blood of their fathers. It was an odd stew of a family, and the compelling piece to Shirley and Van was that they were linked by far more than blood and name. They actually lived together, all ten of them, ostensibly under their mother's care. That is, insofar as a drug-addicted, alcoholic mother with a gambling problem can reasonably expect to care for her ten children.

When their living situation was reported to the police, the ten siblings were sharing a small two-bedroom house in downtown Phoenix with five cousins, all minors—they were all cramped into a hideously unkempt living space and left to mostly fend for themselves. A boyfriend of the mother's sister was supposedly looking after them one weekend while the two mothers were out gambling, and he grew weary at about the same time he grew a conscience. He called the police, and what they found was enough to tug at almost any heart. There were dirty diapers all over the place—even on top of a high-chair tray. There were filthy pots and pans piled eye-high in the kitchen, garbage flies buzzing through every room, and nothing but sour milk in the refrigerator. In fact, when CPS officials came to collect the kids, Donicio, then all of three years old, was sipping from a bottle of spoiled milk.

Frank, the eldest, later told me what it was like living under his mother's "care."

He recalls, "She'd leave us for days, and sometimes weeks. Even when she was there, she wasn't *really* there. I had to be the father to my brothers and sisters. My sister Teresa was like a mother. She did the cooking and the cleaning. When I was about 12, I realized that I needed to find a way to bring money into the family, so I started stealing—video game players, radios, whatever I could find—and I'd turn around and sell them. My mother was never there, and we needed to eat, so I had to do what I had to do. Then I'd go out and buy food and clothing. Whatever we needed. If there was money left over, we'd go to the movies, or to a carnival."

Soon, the thought of all ten children being together again was all Shirley and Van could think about. They'd gotten into this thing with the basic idea of trying to keep a family together, and here they were, right in the middle of the biggest family they'd ever encountered. It was the last thing they'd expected, but they weren't about to look away.

The reunion went well, but it wasn't enough to keep a family together, so Shirley and Van got together with Jean Peirce and decided to make it a monthly affair. Then they went to work trying to get the two youngest siblings, Veronica, then four, and little Doni, placed into their foster care. With Shauna and Michael gone to live with their father, there was room in the Hughes's family quota for two more, and Jean Peirce saw to it that the move happened quickly. She was a true advocate for these kids, and saw in Shirley and Van the kind of lifeline they desperately needed. The truth was, the children had become wards of the state when Veronica and Doni were little more than toddlers, and it was important to them to establish a link with their older brothers and sisters. They were too young to remember back to when they were all together.

A few months later, at a staffing meeting, Jean Peirce put it to Van straight out: "Would you and Shirley consider adopting all ten kids?" she wanted to know. Van's first thought was, *Whoa, that's not even a fair question to ask.* What he said was, "Are you crazy? Do you realize what you're asking?" But what he meant was, *Well, we'd been thinking about trying to keep these kids together in a foster-care situation, so maybe it's not as crazy as it seems.* In addition to the five already living under Van's roof, there was the eldest, Frank, who at 16 was separated from the entire clan; and Augustino, then 11 years old; Steven, 13; Asucena, 14; and Teresa, 15, who were all living together with a foster parent they couldn't stand. At the monthly reunions, they told Shirley and Van that they had to ask permission to get something to eat out of the refrigerator. When these four came to Shirley and Van's for a weekend visit, Asucena asked if they could make it a permanent arrangement.

"Are you rich?" the child asked Van, as she was getting ready to leave.

Van thought about this for a while before offering his answer. "Yes," he finally said, "but not in the way you probably mean."

So on the one hand, Van dismissed the notion of a full-set adoption out of hand, but on the other, he took it home with him, somewhere in the back of his thinking. Shirley, too, kept coming back to the notion, especially as the mother's rights to the children were about to be severed, and a push for adoption would be put in place. According to federal law, since the kids were part Pasqueyaqui Indian, CPS and DES had to first seek a home for them within the tribe. If no one in the tribe was willing to adopt, the search would be opened to all Native Americans. In early 1997, a Cherokee couple in another state indicated that they might be willing to adopt all ten children (they would later change their minds and offer to take in only five), and the thought of "their" kids moving out of state to live with people they'd never even met was deeply unsettling to Van and Shirley.

"How could anybody take these kids in without knowing them?" Shirley wonders now. "Even if they had a good heart and their motives were pure, how could I let these strangers undo all the work we'd done for these kids? How could I let them leave the state? I'd never see them again."

Shirley and Van sat down and made a list for and against adoption. Once again, Van kept coming back to his poor childhood. "I realized that if we had to eat a hundred-pound sack of potatoes and some beans each month, we could do this," he says. They reconfigured their four-bedroom house in their heads, trying to imagine where to put so many children. They could turn the dining room into a bedroom, and convert the garage into a bedroom, and find a way to get by with only two and a half bathrooms. One by one, they crossed the arguments against adoption off their list. They could make the house work. They'd stretch their budget. For a time, they worried that at 50 they were too old to take on a young family. Would they live to see all of them grow up? Would they be a burden to the children later on in life? Would they be able to give them everything they'd need? These arguments, too, didn't really hold. They weren't *that* old. They'd have whatever time they were given, and they'd make the best of the time they had.

Finally, Shirley and Van decided they had no choice but to adopt the children. Five of them were already living in the house, and they loved them as much as if they'd been their own.

They decided to put it to a vote—the kids'. They made hasty arrangements with Jean Peirce to bring the oldest five over for a family meeting disguised as a pizza party, and the kids voted unanimously to throw in with the Hugheses. The oldest five were leery, but they saw the trust and strong attachments their younger siblings enjoyed, and they wanted some of that for themselves. They didn't believe in it, necessarily, but they wanted it just the same.

Now, nearly four years later, they're one sprawling, loving, hardworking, multicultural American family. "The honeymoon is over," Shirley allows. "This is a real family, with all the moodiness and attitude and craziness and trust. We're not tiptoeing around each other anymore." They've even added another brother and sister—Ellery, 20; and Shauna, 19—to the equation. They're Navajo Indian friends of some of the older children who needed a nurturing home. As if ten kids weren't enough.

There's no such thing as a typical day in the Hughes's household, but things start to happen as early as five o'clock in the morning. That's when Shirley sets her alarm so she can get up and fix breakfast and get the kids out of the house and off to school. Van usually sleeps in—he works the swing shift, in security—so it falls to Shirley to get things moving. She wakes the kids in shifts, according to the bus schedule. The first to go is Ellery, who's up at 5:30 to catch an early bus to college; then the high school kids tumble out of bed in 15-minute intervals (to leave time for showers), followed by the elementary schoolers, and finally by the junior high schoolers. (The youngest kids bathe at night to alleviate the strain on the Hughes's two 40-gallon hot-water tanks.) Breakfast is anything from scrambled eggs or pancakes, to cereal and toast. "Whatever they want," Shirley says, "I'm happy to make for them, but I hate it when they ask for eggs, because no one in this house eats eggs the same way."

The house is relatively quiet from about 9 A.M. until 2:30, save for the constant whir of the washer and dryer, when the first batch of kids starts to trickle in from school. A couple of the older kids hold after-school jobs, and they don't get home until 6:30. On some nights, Asucena doesn't get home until ten from her training detail at the police academy. About the only night they manage to sit down to dinner as a family is Friday—pizza night, courtesy of a three-year donation from the local Little Caesar's. "They know us by heart over there," Shirley explains. "Large cheese, large pepperoni, large ham and pineapple, large combination, large pepperoni and black olives, large hamburger."

Shopping is done in bulk, usually built around a monthly trip to CostCo, or to the nearest Air Force base about an hour away. Grocery bills from these big shopping excursions run around $1,500, but Shirley's also back and forth to the local market a couple times each week for fresh milk and bread and other perishables. "We make a lot of big batches," she explains, of the typical Hughes fare. "I never realized how big some pots can be until we had all these kids."

Homework is probably the busiest task, and Shirley and Van have it set up so that the older kids help tutor the younger kids. Van laid it out for the kids from the very beginning that education was important—and the key to household privileges—and so far everyone is thriving. Naturally, some do better than others—six are in special education programs with various learning disabilities—but all are doing better than before, better than anyone expected.

Sunday mornings, the family piles into various cars in the Hughes fleet and heads for church—all, that is, except for Frank, who chooses to stay home. "That's just fine," says Shirley. "He came with us once or twice, but he pulled this attitude on us, and I just don't have the patience for that in church. We're not about to force him. He's the oldest, the other kids look up to him, and if they see him pull that kind of thing in church, it'll trickle down."

Van credits Shirley with turning around the life of each and every one of their adopted children. "She's got a gift from God," he says, "the way she can talk to these kids. Someone asked me one day, 'Who's the greatest person you know?' And I said without hesitation that it was my wife. I may not always treat her that way, but she is."

Of course, from where I sit, it doesn't seem like Shirley would have had much of a chance with these kids if there wasn't a good man like Van at her side—every step of the way.

❀ ❀ ❀

"Are you rich?" the child asked Van.
"Yes," he finally said, "but not in
the way you probably mean."

The Hughes family celebrates
Father's Day 2001.

High hopes for a new tomorrow.

CHAPTER TWO

Rare Birds

Sometimes it takes a tragic turn to shake loose the cobwebs and complacency from our day-to-day lives and remind us of the riches that surround us in silent abundance. Anyway, that's how it's been for me. When my marriage ended, when my kids struggled through one piece of adolescence or another, when my doctors handed down what should have been a devastating diagnosis . . . each time I've been thrown in my adult life, I've been picked up by good and caring friends and family. It's left me thinking that we can get through anything as long as we have the love and support of others.

This is not some watered-down Hallmark sentiment to me. I believe it deeply. I see evidence of the healing powers of love and friendship on my show every time a guest sheds a tear, triumphs unexpectedly, or negotiates a difficult patch. And I see it in the headlines and stories that make their way into our office. Take Ian O'Gorman, for example, a California kid if ever there was one, made to walk a hard road that would have been much tougher if he'd had to go it alone.

About the last thing on Ian's mind when he came back from an awesome afternoon of wave-running on San Diego's Mission Bay was getting sick. It was New Year's Day, and he was at the front end of a month-long school break, looking forward to a whole bunch of time at the beach with his friends and family, gearing up for baseball season, and basically living the kind of active, care-free outdoor life folks outside sunny California can only dream about. He was ten years old, without a worry in the world.

And then, it was the strangest thing, he started to get these intense stomach pains, and he threw up. It began that night, after spending the day on the water, and the pain would come on Ian in a rush. It was like nothing he had ever felt before—like a long, slow punch in the gut. Every day, for the next couple of days, it was the same thing. He'd be fine for a while, for the most part, and then the pain would find him, and then he'd start throwing up again. For a week, things continued in this way, and each time the pain returned, Ian and his parents worried a little bit more. There was the powerful discomfort, and the powerlessness of not knowing what was behind it.

Finally, after a few days too many, Ian's mom took him to the doctor. The doctor tested him for a parasite, thinking that maybe he'd gotten something like salmonella poisoning, and when the test came back positive, the doctor started him on antibiotics. The medicine should have chased the symptoms away within a couple of days, but another week went by and Ian was still throwing up, still being all but knocked over with these rushes of pain, still vomiting. He still hadn't missed any school—in Southern California, on a year-round schedule, Ian went to school two months on, two months off—but it was enough already. This kind of pain, this kind of uncertainty . . . it was off the charts, like nothing in anyone's experience. Ian tried to describe it, but he couldn't come up with the right words. His doctors went from thinking it was a lingering reaction to some unseen parasite, to thinking that maybe there was an infection that was causing his stools to be irregular (and prescribing him laxatives), to ordering up some serious tests. They looked at everything. Whatever it was, they'd figure it out, and in the meantime, Ian and his folks would just have to muddle through.

From Ian's perspective, though, *whatever it was* did not at that point include cancer. "I never thought about anything like that," he says now. "I was just a kid, and that's not a kid's thinking. I'm sure the doctors were thinking about it, and I'm sure my parents were worried, but I just thought of it as me being sick and a whole bunch of people trying to figure out what was making me sick."

During an upper GI series, doctors noticed something blocking Ian's intestine and made hasty arrangements for surgery at Children's Hospital in San Diego. It was meant to be a one-hour procedure, but it ended up taking four hours. Ian's parents were in the waiting room, going quietly crazy, wondering what was taking so long, dreading what the surgeon might find. Every worst-case scenario bounced through their heads.

The surgery revealed that Ian's right kidney wasn't functioning, so another surgery was scheduled for a few days later, and it was during this second surgery that doctors discovered and removed a tumor inside Ian's small intestine. The surgeon later told Ian that the tumor was the size of an orange.

So now he knew. Cancer. Non-Hodgkins lymphoma, actually, with a fairly good chance of survival. The course of treatment was nine weeks of chemotherapy, to be administered on an outpatient basis, beginning as soon as possible.

"I was ten years old," Ian recalls, "and my parents were completely flipping out, but I was only flipping a little bit. You have to realize, I was on so much medication that I don't know that I could really think about it. Plus, you know, I was pretty young. I cried a little when the doctor told me. I knew what it was, what it meant, and I asked a bunch of questions. 'What kind of cancer is it? How bad is it? Am I gonna die?' Those kinds of things."

One of the social workers came by Ian's hospital room to explain some of the side effects of the chemotherapy. Ian's parents were visiting at the time, along with his good friend Taylor and his brother, Cheyne, and they all listened as the social worker explained how Ian's hair was going to fall out, and how a lot of kids actually shave it off before their first treatment so that it doesn't come out in clumps. She talked about how some young patients are ostracized by their peers for walking around school without their hair, but Ian's buddy and his brother had a different take.

Ian explains, "They just sat there, listening to all this, and one of them said, 'Hey, you know what? We're gonna shave our heads, too!' It wasn't any kind of big deal at first. They just wanted to show me they were with me, that even though I was the one who was sick, we could be in this thing together. You know, if someone wanted to stare at me or point at me, they'd have to stare and point at them, too. I thought, *Hey, that's kinda cool.*"

It turned out to be a much bigger deal than anyone in that hospital room could have imagined. When Ian went back to school after a two-and-a-half-week stint at Children's Hospital, he was surprised to see a note posted to his classroom door—a sign-up sheet, really, for other kids wanting to shave their heads in support of Ian. He had no idea that the notion had spread beyond his hospital room, but there was a pretty long list of names on there, as Ian remembers it, and when the class got going, it was all anyone wanted to talk about. Ian's fifth-grade teacher, Jim Alter, told his students that if they were planning to shave down for Ian, he would shave down, too, and a couple days later, the entire class went to the local barber shop to make good on their pledge.

"We got there, and there were all these TV cameras and newspaper reporters," Ian says. "It was crazy. We hadn't expected any attention from this; it was just something we all felt like doing, but one of the kids said something, and someone called the local paper, and the whole thing kinda spread. I wasn't shaved down yet, so I took my turn with everyone else. There were five chairs in the barber shop, so five of us sat down at a time, and we all had our heads shaved. Mr. Alter, too. There was even a girl in our class who wanted to do it. She sat down in the chair and was all ready to go, but her mother was there and talked her out of it.

"The next day, back at school, Mr. Alter had a sign on his door that said, 'You make me proud, my little bald eagles,' and the name just took. After that, we were known as the Bald Eagles. There were 13 of us to start out, but then other kids started hearing about it, and they shaved their heads, too. Kids in other classes. Kids in other grades. Friends of mine, or friends of my brother's. There was a whole bunch of us."

Meanwhile, Ian began his chemo treatments with great hesitation. He'd been fitted with a kind of portable catheter underneath his skin, which would allow him to continue his normal activities. He didn't know what to expect. He was told that the treatments might leave him feeling nauseated and fatigued, that he might not be able to stay in school throughout his nine-week course of treatment, and that he would have his good and bad days. Still, hesitation or not, he was determined not to let his illness derail him from his routines. His mother scheduled his treatments on school days, and the plan was for him to go to school in the morning, get his chemo around midday, and return to school in the afternoon. He expected to get sick, but the sickness never came. "It affects people differently," he explains, "and in my case, I was lucky. The way it worked, with the porto-cath, I was able to play baseball, go to the beach, and do all the things I usually did. I don't think I missed a game or a practice the whole time."

The only way to tell that Ian O'Gorman was any different from the dozen or so other bald-headed boys in his class was the way TV cameras and reporters tended to follow him around wherever he went.

"The whole media thing didn't die down for a couple months," he says. "*People* magazine, *Good Morning America*, a crew from Japanese television. Every television station in San Diego. All the papers. These people kept following me on the way to school, on the way to the hospital. They knew my schedule. They were everywhere. They even had these news helicopters hovering over my house."

And it wasn't just the media that responded. Every day in class, someone from the school office would wheel in boxes of letters from people all over the country, people who were touched by the story of Ian and the Bald Eagles, people who shaved their own heads in solidarity, people who had done their own battles with cancer and wished like hell that they'd had good friends to support them in the way that Ian's friends had lined up for him.

Mr. Alter read some of the letters to the class, and the daily drama almost became a part of the curriculum. Check that: In many ways, it became the most *important* part of the curriculum. There was even a fax transmission from some guy on a boat, traveling around the world. How the story found him, in the middle of the ocean, Ian couldn't imagine.

Ask Ian today why he thinks his story and the rallying-around of his friends and classmates struck such a chord with people all over the world, and he'll offer up a thoughtful, dead-on response: "People's image of kids is that they're mean to each other," he reasons, "that they only care about themselves, and this is a rare thing— to see elementary school kids showing support for each other. That's not the picture most people have. Usually, it's the opposite. There's all of this finger-pointing and name-calling. I had all these nurses and social workers telling me I was gonna be made to feel different, and then these 10- and 11-year-old kids show this sign of affection. This real acceptance. Total acceptance. It was just amazing, unbelievable, and I think it took people by surprise, a little bit, to see kids behaving like this."

Well, he's right about that, but I can't help thinking that there was another piece to Ian's story that people found so compelling, and that piece was Ian himself. Throughout his entire ordeal, he kept a smile on his face, and a winning outlook. He refused to let his cancer slow him down. Granted, a lot of folks take a winning outlook into their cancer treatment, only to be beaten back by the ravages of the chemotherapy, but Ian was more than lucky in this regard.

I've always believed that things happen for a reason—good things and bad—and here, Ian was cast as a kind of magnet for this overflow of good feeling and positive energy. He kept playing ball, riding his wave-runner, going to school, and graciously fielding the same questions from reporters, until finally he emerged as a kind of poster boy for standing up and doing the right thing. For supporting your friends. For riding out the bad patches and holding on for the good ones. For refusing to quit, or to bend.

When the chemo treatments were finished, Ian went with his whole family for his CAT scan to see if he was clean. His parents; his brother, Cheyne; his little sister, Mackenzie . . . all of them huddled together, waiting for the doctor to come out with the news. Hoping. Praying.

Ian knew deep down that he had beaten this thing when he looked at the doctor as he approached with the news that the worst was over. "I could tell on his face that he wasn't coming over to tell us something bad," Ian recalls. "He wasn't smiling, but I could tell, and then he told us, and we all had this happy cry, and I wished my friends could have been there with me. Because, really, it was the whole distraction, the whole media circus, that kept me from thinking about the cancer, that kept me from thinking about the chemo. And it was all thanks to them. There was always something going on, and I was never made to feel different in any kind of bad way. Different, yeah, because it was me at the center of all this attention, but it had such a positive spin to it. It was a bunch of guys trying to do something so I wouldn't feel left out, and I ended up being made to feel special instead."

When he was in the eighth grade, a couple years after Ian thought he had the cancer beat, the same symptoms started to kick up in his stomach. The same intense pain. The same nausea. Ian had been going back every six months to double-check that the cancer hadn't returned, and his last check had been clean, but he was fairly freaked just the same. This time, he was old enough to put these symptoms into scary perspective. This time, he knew what they meant. It turned out, though, that there wasn't much to worry about beyond a few lingering complications from his initial surgery. There was some scar tissue that had wrapped around his small intestine, cutting off his circulation. There were some hours of real uncertainty in there, some rallying-around of his good friends, but once the doctors determined the cause of the pain, they were able to go in and remove the tissue and the damaged section of intestine, and within a couple weeks, Ian was back playing ball. The surgeon used the same incision from the first time—nine inches long—and Ian healed quick enough to finish out his Pony League season.

The media swirl eventually calmed, but not before a local woman reacted to all the fuss. Her name was Carolyn Bechtal, and she was doing some work for the No Fear clothing company, a leading manufacturer of youth-friendly apparel (T-shirts, hats, jeans, etc.). She donated these ball caps with the No Fear logo on the front and "Bald Eagles" stitched on the back, and Ian and his buddies wore them with pride and got to thinking. One thought led to another, and soon Carolyn Bechtal had gotten together with Ian and his dad to get the Bald Eagles Foundation off the ground, a youth-based cancer support network that offers outreach to kids and families going through some of the same challenges Ian had to face. Whatever it takes, that's what they'll do. No matter where it takes them.

"I would have loved to have met someone like me when I was first diagnosed," Ian reasons. "To have seen someone all healthy, playing ball, smiling. To know that he had beaten the cancer. It would have totally made me feel like *I can do this*. So I wind up doing a lot of talking to other kids. I go to them and they get the message, *Hey, I'm alive, and I'm doing well*. There haven't been any other mass shave-ins, not that we know about, but we've helped people with money, directed them to various resources, and gotten them thinking in a positive way."

The good folks at No Fear kicked in a couple thousand ball caps, which Ian and his pals designed. He came across a quote—"Why run when you can fly?"—and asked the company to stitch it on the back, above "Bald Eagles" in small print, and Ian and his friends sold them all over town at $10 a pop. Everyone seemed to want one, and they sold out without too much peddling. The foundation also teamed up with a group of NASCAR drivers and raised over $28,000 from one NASCAR event alone. More fund-raisers are in the works, and Ian's hope, when he gets out of college, is to run the foundation himself—have it make an even broader impact on a national scale. One kid at a time. Whatever it takes.

Amazingly, the Bald Eagles Foundation was able to reach out to another child from the very same elementary school Ian attended. The kid's name is Jeremy Gable, and he was almost exactly the same age Ian was when he first took ill. Same grade in school. Diagnosed with the very same type of cancer. Confronting the same course of treatment. And, inevitably, dealing with some of the same issues. Jeremy's buddies didn't shave down the way Ian's pals did, but they found other ways to show their support, and the nearly graduated Bald Eagles took Jeremy under their "wings" and welcomed him into the fold.

"We were a whole lot older," Ian explains, "but Jeremy was one of us. He beat it the first time, but then it came back a couple years later, and now we're expecting him to beat it again."

For now, college looms for Ian at California State University, Long Beach. Ian's current thinking is that a career in business would be interesting—some kind of job that would let him work at his foundation and continue reaching out to help kids with cancer, and spread the supportive word that even a bad diagnosis can have a good outcome. He's still playing ball, still hangin' at the beach. He's traded baseball for basketball, and captained his high school team during his senior year. At 5'10", he's no towering menace on the floor, but he can pump in three-pointers all day long. He's shot past his five-year, clean-bill-of-health, but he gets a thorough workup every year just to be sure. And his hair has long since grown back, although he's shaved down from time to time when he's felt like it. The Bald Eagles, too, have all weathered their high school years in style—some clean-shaven, some not, but all linked by their spontaneous coming together in adolescence.

"A thing like this, it scares you into making the right decisions," Ian says. "We're all good kids. We've all stayed out of trouble, pretty much. And we still hang out and watch each other's backs. We'll always be good friends. What it taught us, I think, is that you need to live life to the fullest, every day. It taught us that there are good people out there, and that *we are* those good people. We are *all* those good people. What happened to me, to us, touched so many people, because you don't see too many acts of friendship like that. You open up a newspaper and there's violence and killing. There are kids going to school with guns. But this was different. This was positive."

Yes, it was. And yes, it is.

✿ ✿ ✿

AP/Wide World Photos

The Bald Eagles Then: Kneeling: *Jerad Mendonza*; 2nd row: *Chris Chatham* and *Andrew Nydstrom*; 3rd row: *Stephen Schroeder, Paul Teran, Ian O'Gorman, Kyle Pardi, Scott Seblius, Ian McClellan*; 4th row: *Taylor Herber, Erik Holzhauer, James McMillan*

Jay Lee

The Bald Eagles Now: Front row: *Chris Chatham, Ian O'Gorman, Scott Sebelius, Mr. Alter;* Back row: *Carson Smith, Gabe Cornejo, Paul Teran, Erik Holzhauer, Kyle Pardi, James McMillan, and Cheyne O'Gorman*

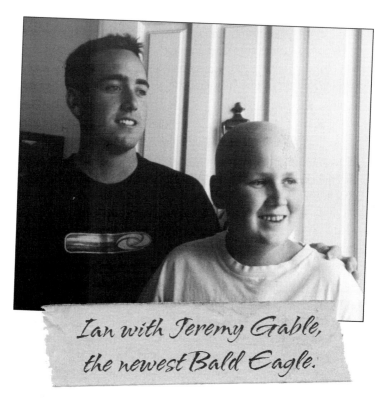

Ian with Jeremy Gable,
the newest Bald Eagle.

Eddie Lama (right) with Daryl Williams and Blondi the dog.

CHAPTER THREE

Great and Small

*A*ll the earth's creatures mean something to Eddie Lama. Two-legged. Four-legged. Fur-coated. Winged, scaled, and shelled. Nothing unusual here, until you find out a little about where Eddie comes from, the kind of life he used to live, the complete 180 he's done to turn his own life around—and, along with it, the lives of hundreds of abused and abandoned dogs, cats, pigs, pigeons, chickens, sheep, goats, and rabbits—and dozens of recovering addicts and ex-cons, who, like himself, have been through hard times and need an opportunity to bring out the goodness that lies within.

In recognition of his passionate and innovative advocacy for animals, Eddie Lama received the Courage of Conscience Award in June of 2001 from the Peace Abbey in Sherborn, Massachusetts. Past recipients of this award have included the likes of Mother Teresa and the Dalai Lama. Pretty exalted company for a construction contractor who grew up poor in a violent Brooklyn neighborhood, a boy who thought animals were vile, disgusting creatures to avoid at all costs. When you follow the steps of his path to the present day and learn all he has overcome, you'll see why no one is more surprised than Eddie that his life has turned out the way it has.

As a kid, making a name for himself with the neighborhood wise guys, Eddie was known for the lengths he'd go to prove a point. By 13 or so, he was engaging in petty criminal activity, brawling, generally making trouble.

"I grew up in a neighborhood where everybody's middle name was The," he half-jokes. "Literally. We had The Rock, The Hammer. Me? I was just Crazy Eddie, and I did a lot of crazy things. I'm not proud of some of the things I did, but I did them. The violence was against our own little criminal element for the most part. We weren't beating up on little old ladies or children, just on each other. It was all about how many heads you rolled, how many goods you pinched off a truck. It was about making a name for yourself, making a reputation. Sometimes people would do things like sneak into the zoo at night to hurt the animals, just to show off. Crazy as I was, I never did that, but I didn't give it too much thought either. Everyone in my family felt animals were disgusting."

As the years passed, the consequences of Eddie's choice of "hang-out crowd" turned ugly, and one night, he found himself on the stick end of a shovel, being beaten to a pulp by a group of neighborhood rivals.

"I lay there in the street," he recalls, "and I knew I was gonna die. It was completely out of my experience, what was happening. I'd known guys to get a beating, but nothing had ever gone this far. These people meant to kill me with this shovel, and then they set me on fire. I lay there, conscious, powerless to do anything but keep living, confused and bewildered by the whole thing. I couldn't understand why nobody was calling for help. Nobody ever came to help me, and they left me, thinking I was dead. A doctor at the hospital told me later that they wheeled me in with a tag already on my toe. But I didn't die. They botched the job."

Eddie survived the beating, but he almost didn't survive what came next. He'd always been a heavy drinker—alcohol and drugs were the background music to his growing up—but after the beating, his drinking drastically increased. "My behavior became really hurtful to myself as well as those around me," he remembers, "and I lost a lot of things."

In 1978, Eddie was involved in an incident in a bar that sent him on a five-year hitch to various state correctional facilities. "First time I did real dope was in prison. I'd basically been a drunk all my life, smoked some pot, but heavy drugs I got in the joint." Although he continued to drink, alcohol was hard to come by, and in between binges he found time to read, to give himself the education he felt he never got in high school. Eddie read book after book on all kinds of subjects and discovered an abiding interest in philosophy and mythology. He even challenged himself to learn the meaning of every word in the dictionary.

When Eddie got out in the early 1980s, he was on the edge. He'd learned a lot in prison, but his problems still haunted him. He managed for a time to make a go of things as a hairdresser, and he even met and married a great lady who set him up with his own upscale shop in Brooklyn Heights. But it was downhill from there. He ran through his money, lost his shop, and wound up on the streets, lost in a haze of drink and drugs.

"Alcohol is a great solvent," he observes. "It's a remover. It removed my friends, it removed my family, it removed money out of my wallet. And so I was really left with nothing except me and the drugs and alcohol that I thought at that time were my friends." Even his favorite uncle turned away after he discovered Eddie's needles in his house, where the man's young children could have found them.

"I was pretty down and out," Eddie admits, "but thank God for the people who tried to help, and thank God for my Uncle Sal, because he didn't give up on me. He came around in a car and literally scraped me off the streets of Red Hook and carried me to a rehab facility out in Jersey. Happy Acres, I called it. I don't want to mention the real name of the place, because really it was a lousy place, exploiting drug addicts for insurance money. But that doesn't matter. I was ready. It was my time to make a change."

Eddie got to work on himself, and he reached up to find a helping hand extended from Eddie

Rizzo, a fellow neighborhood tough guy Eddie had met in the joint who'd managed to land a union construction job upon his own release from prison. Eddie Lama just past 30 years old, started working for the same union, low man, breaking concrete. It was, they both admit, a union of former criminals, scoundrels, and scalawags, but hard work was hard work. As it was, the work wasn't steady, but it was something, and Eddie set himself up in a tiny one-room flat in a run-down building, proud to be able to make the $55 weekly rent.

"It was a miserable place, but I was grateful to my landlady. She, too, was in recovery, and she gave a number of us a safe place to explore our newfound gift of sobriety. I'd come home from work, all filthy and dead and dusted out from chipping, into this pretty depressing room, and I thought to myself, Okay, Eddie. You're on the right path."

Yes, he was, and that path would eventually take him to a job overseeing an independent construction crew for a local contractor. He had no idea what he was doing at first, but he learned. "People took advantage of my inexperience. My crew would install 16 windows, I'd come back and tell my boss we did that many, and he'd flip, saying we should have done 40. I had no frame of reference, so I had to learn."

And so, he learned, and within 18 months, he was all but running the small company. When his supervisor split to run his own firm, Eddie had to make a decision: follow his boss to this new enterprise, or stay on with the company that had been good to him and that had given him a fresh start. "I didn't like the way this guy split off," he says. "It was hostile, and I was on this new path with my sobriety and didn't want to be in that kind of environment, so I stayed. Little did I know, the guy I stayed with, he turned out to be a big crook. Dropping little brown bags off to people, working all these side deals. I didn't want to be a part of that. Drinking, doping, everything. I wanted to stay clean, all the way. So I bailed. I was outta there. At the time, I was making good money. Twenty-five hundred a week. Great money. Clean money. This guy wasn't clean, but I was clean, staying sober every day."

Over time, Eddie built a new kind of reputation as an independent aluminum, concrete, and glass contractor—"best in the city," he says—and part of that reputation was his integrity. "I don't believe in contracts. Of course, you gotta have 'em in today's world, but I follow the spirit of the contract, not the letter. I don't nickel-and-dime people. People liked the way I work. If I told them I'd do something, I'd do it. Like Aristotle said, a good man keeps his promises. In the long run, it will benefit you physically, mentally and spiritually. The energy you put out is the energy you get back."

As his years of sobriety stacked up, Eddie began to see beyond the horizon of his own problems. One day, a chance encounter with a desperate homeless man reminded him of all he'd been through on his way to the bottom, and in that moment his heart opened. "I remember at the late age of 34 or 35, I actually felt another's pain to the extent where I cried. I cried for another's pain, that was a breakthrough for me. And it felt strange, it felt good. I wanted to do more. So I joined different humanitarian organizations that dealt with starving children and tortured political prisoners, things of that nature, the plight of humanity. I gave money and wrote letters, and I wanted to be more active."

Everything was starting to change, but Eddie's growing circle of compassion was not yet complete. In spite of all he was learning, he still maintained the disdain for animals he learned as a boy. He avoided his friends' dogs and cats like the plague, and would even cross the street to avoid a stray animal. The only thing he enjoyed about animals was eating them at his favorite table at the Knickerbocker steakhouse. Then, something happened that would change his life forever.

It all started with a beautiful woman who asked Eddie to baby-sit her kitten. Eddie didn't care about the kitten, but he really wanted to get a date, so he agreed to bring the animal into his house. At first he was repelled, but then he started to get curious about the kitten. The way she yawned and stretched and chased after a tossed ball fascinated him, and he suddenly realized that he'd never had a chance before to interact with an animal. It struck him that everything he'd thought about animals was completely wrong, and it was not long before the kitten started acting like his newfound friend, and Eddie was, as he likes to say, "smitten by a kitten."

Not long after, the same lady asked Eddie to foster a stray cat, and this new cat became even more of a friend than the last, eventually causing Eddie to break his two-pack-a-day cigarette habit. "I coulda sworn I heard him cough," Eddie explains, "and I realized that this secondhand smoke couldn't be good for his little cat lungs, right? I mean, if he could speak, or somehow tell me his thoughts, he'd have told me he didn't want to be harmed in this way. It's wild, I know, but this is how I started to see things."

Then came another stray named Bagel, whom Eddie rescued from starvation. Once he took the cat home, and held him, and gently squeezed his leg all the way down to the foot, he couldn't shake thinking how much Bagel's leg reminded him of a chicken drumstick. He got this picture in his head, and it stuck. The moment he made this connection was the moment he stopped eating meat. Forever.

"They eat cats regularly in some cultures, and we're appalled by it," Eddie now reasons. "Why is that? I'd always loved a good steak, it's delicious, but once I had that connection with the cat, I couldn't take another bite. Steak, chicken, bacon—even fish. Cows and pigs and chickens, they've got emotions, same as us. They move about, same as us. They get cold or tired or hungry, same as us. They feel pain, just like we feel pain. And it hurts me to see my friends being eaten. It hurts me, knowing what these animals go through, in these factory farms and slaughterhouses. I think about how I felt when I was getting beaten, and no one spoke up or tried to help me. I don't judge you if you're a meat-eater, but I find it difficult to be around when people are eating the cooked remains of a once-living sentient being. I can't put it out of my mind."

Now, it's one thing to allow a small domesticated animal into your heart in such a way that it changes your outlook, but it's quite another to let it transform your entire existence. At first, Eddie's turnaround was self-directed. He stopped eating meat, dairy, and eggs, and he gave up wearing leather or wool. He stopped using products that had been tested on animals, or supporting businesses that exploited animals in any way. Soon enough, his circle of caring grew to include any number of stray, abandoned, or abused animals that came his way. Friends, and friends of friends, started sending wounded dogs and cats Eddie's way for safe-keeping. He'd dip into his own pocket for veterinary costs and food.

As he spent more time with animals, he identified more with their plight. "I started to make connections between what I'd experienced in jail and the animals. I just know what it feels like to be caged. And you know what?" he laughs. "I probably deserved to be caged. But the animals don't deserve to be. They didn't break any laws, so why are they being punished? It's a horrible thing, to be caged in, to pace back and forth, nowhere to go. At least I had a good lawyer. But there are no lawyers for the pigs, the chimps, the mink caged in misery on fur farms. Life imprisonment, with no chance for parole."

In 1998, with his own money, Eddie founded FaunaVision, a nonprofit organization dedicated to offering a positive vision of the human-animal relationship. Its flagship program was a state-of-the-art multimedia van, which Eddie designed and built to roam the streets of New York City, promoting awareness about the plight of animals. Eddie outfitted the van with two 35-inch color monitors, four high-performance speakers, a scrolling computerized message board, and a cordless public address system. It was a mobile theater, a classroom, and a billboard all in one, and Eddie hoped it would change people's perceptions about how animals are treated. In their first year on the road with the van, Eddie's volunteers distributed more than a quarter-million pieces of animal advocacy literature to passersby.

"Education is the key to change," he explains. "People don't know what's really going on until they see it with their own eyes. My awakening didn't just come out of a cosmic wasteland. It didn't just materialize from nothing. It was all these events that were presented to me. With FaunaVision, we're trying to facilitate that for people on the streets."

In the process of driving all over the city, Eddie began rescuing stray dogs and cats from roadsides and back alleys, the office of his construction company now doubling as a haven for animals. Even Eddie's crew starting getting involved, finding cats on construction sites and taking them in for veterinary care. Eddie's foreman rescued a kitten on the job and named her Snowball. But there wasn't enough space for all the animals, and Eddie soon found himself looking for a better, longer-term solution. He looked north, to the sleepy upstate town of North Branch, New York, in the heart of the Catskills mountain region, where he purchased an old dairy farm that he hoped to transform into an animal sanctuary and adoption center. He dubbed the place Oasis, for that's what it was: a vision in the desert, a place of refuge in a dark, uncertain world, a sign of hope.

Today, Oasis Sanctuary is home to hundreds of abused and abandoned animals. Many of the dogs and cats in residence have been rescued from the streets of New York City. All of the farm animals have been saved from the butcher's knife.

"Each animal at Oasis has a name, a sad story, and a happy ending," says Eddie. "We're not interested in warehousing animals. As beautiful as it is up here, it's a pale second to a loving home. Our preference is to place these animals with individual families, and we do that by word-of-mouth, advertising, whatever it takes."

Oasis also promotes public awareness of animal issues throughout the Catskills region, with a no-fee adoption program, a subsidized spay/neuter program, and a volunteer outreach program for area school children and mentally challenged adults. Volunteers help around the farm by walking the dogs, playing with the cats, feeding the pigs, and cleaning their living areas. They also learn about the proper care and handling of animals, as well as the virtues and benefits of a vegetarian lifestyle.

Eddie is backboned in these efforts by his old pal Eddie Rizzo. Lama put Rizzo to work driving the FaunaVision media van, and softened his hardened, meat-eating heart one night over dinner, with a vivid description of the brutality suffered by pigs on their way to the slaughterhouse. Now, Eddie Rizzo is a card-carrying vegan, and a full-time volunteer-in-residence at Oasis, overseeing the farm and coordinating "Crazy" Eddie Lama's other grand plan—the safe-housing and nurturing of indigent, recovering alcoholics and drug addicts, who come to the sanctuary to live and work in its nonviolent, drug-free vegetarian environment. These "guests" receive free room and board on the farm, and a weekly salary for the various chores assigned to them. In addition to their work, they are also required to attend local substance abuse programs at least three times a week.

Eddie Lama never set out to establish a cutting-edge rehabilitation facility, but that's what he's done in his own seat-of-the-pants way. He's got his own ideas, and with the success of his construction business, he's got the money to put those ideas into play. Here, his inspired thinking is that the symbiotic relationship between these disenfranchised, disempowered animals and these disenfranchised, disempowered human beings will yield great benefits for each.

That they'll come together through the common bond of suffering, and in many cases, rejection. And so far, they have. It's a strangely wonderful thing to see, these recovering addicts from urban settings who've never been around animals their entire lives, forging simple, pure, trusting relationships with animals in need.

"When people are active in their addiction," says Eddie, "they get outta touch with their own feelings. They lose awareness of the pain others are feeling. Some of the men in our program are just like I was. They've never cared for another being before. I see how it changes as they go to their meetings and take care of the animals. Some of the critters are sick or disabled, and I see the guys start to take special care with them. They become less self-absorbed, and know they're making a difference. I've seen it help their ability to make peace with people they've hurt in the past, and bring a new sense of self-respect. It's a beautiful thing to watch happen."

Already, he hears from other agencies around the country who are looking to model their own program on Oasis, or to place people into the Oasis program, even as Eddie worries about "institutionalizing" the idea. "I'd like to keep it organic," he says, "connected. I hear from old friends, 'Hey, this guy's trying to stay sober, can you help him out?' Those are the guys we want."

At Oasis, program guests go by the rules—or they go home. Rule one, naturally, is that they must continue with their supervised programs of recovery. The second rule is that they can only stay 90 days. Any longer, Eddie feels, and they'll see the sanctuary as a crutch, instead of a place to jump-start or redirect their lives.

"You don't want to give them the feeling that this is forever. It's nothing I learned in books, or from experts in the field. It's common sense. It's what I felt myself when I was rehabbing. After three months, you're doing okay, you can step off and do something else. Move forward. Or, maybe you're someone who's become real passionate about the work we're doing here, become inspired by it, then maybe you can stay on, but then that's not rehab. Then it's a job."

Rule three, they have to respect the philosophy. "We're motivated by a principle here," he explains. "We're not just doing this for the sake of doing this. Our mission is to not exploit animals as much as we can, and one of the simplest ways is to not eat them. Do I expect every one of these guys to become a vegetarian? No, but while they're here, they do things the Oasis way. A Burger King wrapper in one of my trucks? That's contraband up here. That's like bringing in drugs. That's how strongly we feel about not killing animals."

Eddie's ethic of compassion now colors every aspect of his life. Listen to Eddie on what it means to traffic in some of the stolen goods that abound in the construction industry: "There's a lot of hot stuff in my business. Stolen equipment, stolen tools. I get approached all the time. Some other guy might think, Oh, that's a good deal. It's already stolen. It's not like I'm stealing it. If I don't buy it, someone else will. But not me. I don't want it, because if you think that way, then everything becomes okay. The cow's already dead, so what's the difference if you eat a hamburger? Well, the difference is, if all of us stopped eating meat, there wouldn't be a dead cow. If nobody bought hot tools, there wouldn't be a market for them. I don't care how much money you'd save, you lose a part of your soul. You're making a deal with the devil as part of your payment plan. So, yeah, one man can always make a difference. The only thing you can leave on this earth is your legacy. When you die, you have nothing. It's not at all like that bumper sticker, 'Whoever dies with the most toys wins.' That's not it at all. It's whoever dies with the most serenity."

Eddie is Brooklyn all the way, right down to the accent, and as serene as he may be on the inside, on the outside he can't go two minutes without action, whether it's working a deal on his cell phone or stopping at a hanging length of horizontal piping to do some pull-ups. He's a wiry bundle of energy and ideas—and these days, most of each are directed toward helping the wounded animals and people that cross his path.

Recently, Eddie has been able to carry his message beyond the city streets through an award-winning film called The Witness: A Tribe of Heart Documentary, which has helped people all over the country learn about his remarkable personal journey. Being the subject of a film and receiving recognition such as the Courage of Conscience Award has underscored for Eddie the importance of staying "right sized," of keeping the focus on principles and not his personality.

"It's funny that I should share an award with the Dalai Lama," Eddie laughs, "because I've made a running joke out of our shared name. I always say to people, 'I'm not the Dalai Lama, I'm Eddie Lama.' Because I'm not a saintly person. I happen to believe in nonviolence toward animals, so in that regard, it is true that I'm a pacifist. But don't put me on any kind of pedestal."

So how does Eddie Lama reconcile the man he was with the man he's become? For now, it's enough that he and his buddy Rizzo, two former tough guys, have put their street smarts together in the service of building a true oasis—for all manner of lost souls. Oasis Sanctuary really is a thing to see, this proof of what's possible when people find their path and stick to it with everything they've got, this retrofitted dairy farm with an observation deck to allow potential adopters to view dogs at play in extensive open air runs, animal-washing stations, feed bins, rabbits, goats, gobbling turkeys, and free-ranging chickens crossing the town road that bisects the sanctuary as if they owned the joint—which, thanks to Eddie, they really do.

❋ ❋ ❋

"We're not interested in warehousing animals . . . as beautiful as it is up here, it's a pale second to a loving home."

Eddie with resident goat "Frank Zappa."

Eddie with some of his friends.

From left: Oasis co-founder Eddie Rizzo, James La Veck, Eddie Lama, and an Oasis visitor.

"*Of course, I can look back and see how strange it must have seemed.*"

CHAPTER FOUR

Running on Empty

I've been at this talk-show game a good long while, and before that I visited a couple hundred high schools and youth groups as a motivational speaker, and in all my years working with troubled kids and families, I've interviewed a clinic's worth of young girls struggling with one kind of eating disorder or another. It's one of our great cultural regrets, the way so many of our kids let a shared anxiety over physical appearance rule so many aspects of their lives.

According to the American Psychiatric Association, between 5 and 10 percent of all young women in the United States have a distorted body image, low self-esteem in regard to the way they look, or a preoccupation with becoming thin. Of that group, about 10 percent fit all the criteria for a clinical diagnosis of anorexia nervosa. I even saw a segment on a national morning TV show recently that said a good percentage of eight-year-old girls have either dieted or expressed concern about their weight. Eight-year-olds! So it's not surprising that the subject has come up in all kinds of ways over the course of my career.

Anorexia nervosa, for those of you who may be unfamiliar with the term, is a potentially life-threatening mental illness that causes an intense fear of weight gain, and a false perception of weight and body shape, usually resulting in an unnatural obsession with food and dieting. Now, there have been recorded cases of self-starvation throughout history, but this illness has become more and more common in contemporary Western society as we increasingly emphasize and embrace a certain physical ideal. Thin is in—in Hollywood, on Madison Avenue, and wherever else our tastemakers and trendsetters gather to establish our cultural norms—and fat is out. What gets lost in the balance is the message that it's okay to stand apart from the crowd, to follow our own predetermined paths. To be who we are.

I'm telling you all of this to set the scene for my first meeting with Sarah Ezzie, a remarkable young woman from the West Side of Cleveland who first appeared on my show as a 68-pound teenager on the long road to recovery from this all-too-common disorder. I'm happy to report that she's now a thriving 125-pound college student at John Carroll University in Ohio (and a certified kickboxing instructor, to boot!). But at the time, she was struggling. Still, she was brave enough and gracious enough to appear on the show with a panel of young women going through some of the same difficult motions, and I saw in Sarah the face of our troubled society.

The thing about Sarah was that she didn't fit the profile of the typical anorexic. She wasn't standing in front of a mirror trying to look like a flavor-of-the-month model, or flipping through the pages of a fashion magazine griping about how she'd never fit into this or that particular outfit. Not at all. She was a card-carrying tomboy, a full-fledged jock. She wasn't especially into boys, clothes, or any kind of physical ideal. She didn't care about her hair, her hips, or her shoes. All she wanted was to play basketball or football with her two older brothers, or kick their butts in pizza-eating contests. She had a long list of good friends, and she was the star of her school soft-ball team. About the only obsession Sarah had regarding food was health-related: She was a veg-etarian by personal choice, and at an early age she found that she was careful about the kinds of foods she took into her body. She had a hearty appetite, and she always felt that she was eating enough to satisfy it, although in retrospect she realizes that she wasn't taking in nearly enough fat or protein for an active adolescent.

By the eighth grade, though, Sarah found herself cutting back on all kinds of foods, healthy or otherwise. Grocery shopping became an obsessive chore, as she stopped before every label to consider calories, carbs, and sodium and fat levels. She started driving her poor mother crazy. Sarah wouldn't eat unless she chose the food herself, and she wouldn't choose the food without first reading every label on the shelf. It took forever just to get down one aisle!

"Of course, I can look back and see how strange it must have seemed," Sarah says now, "but at the time I just thought I was being careful about what I was eating. Everything had to be low-fat. Low in calories. Nothing artificial. What happened, though, was that I started eating less and less. It wasn't anything I thought about or planned. It just happened. My parents both worked, my brothers were hardly around, and we never really ate dinner together as a family. My mother would prepare meals for us, which we were supposed to take from the fridge whenever we got home, but more and more I'd find myself just taking an English muffin and going to my room. Being by myself. Locking the door and writing poetry. That was my thing back in those days. I hung out with my friends less and less. I packed my own lunch for school, and I started to just take an apple with me, and pretty soon I wasn't even eating that. One or two bites, and that was it."

Eventually, not eating took its toll on Sarah— at one point, she even stopped drinking water! She slipped from an already-tiny 85 pounds to a dangerously thin 70 pounds. For a while, she was able to mask her weight loss with big, baggy clothes, but her parents and friends couldn't help but notice. Fifteen pounds may not seem like a lot for a kid to lose, but when you're starting from a base of 85, it's considerable. Even her softball coach took note. Sarah had always been a star athlete among her crowd, and she went from being a key member of the girl's softball team—batting cleanup, playing a level of game that belied her small stature—to barely having the strength to muscle the ball out of the infield.

Up until this time, Sarah was obsessive about her schoolwork, tallying straight *A*s, and here she turned that same obsession on herself. She strived to understand what was happening to her, to have it make sense, but she kept drawing blanks. She knew what anorexia was and what it meant, but she figured that there had to be something else going on. Anorexia was for the self-centered girls she read about in news magazines, for the ones lacking in the self-esteem department. Sarah was fine with the way she looked. As far as she could tell, she had no self-image problems. Body-image concerns were never a big deal in her house, and they certainly hadn't become major issues overnight. No, about the only real change she could discern was the shift in her family dynamic once her brother Ryan left the house for the University of Miami at Ohio. And now that her other brother Ray was about to leave for Ohio University, things were all of a sudden a whole lot different than they'd ever been before. The house was often empty, and when her parents were around, they tended to fight. There were money troubles, and all kinds of related tensions. Sarah's friends at school moved about with the kind of ease and confidence she could only resent; their lives at home were calm and predictable; *her* life was up in the air and all over the place.

Sarah's world seemed for the first time to spin out of control, and she guesses now that she seized on this obsession with food as perhaps the one thing in her life she *could* control. "I didn't understand it then," she reflects, "but I think that's what it was. Me, trying to get a handle on all these things in the only way I could."

On one day that she'll never forget, her father brought a scale into the kitchen and hollered for Sarah to come downstairs to weigh herself. He wasn't loving or gentle about it, she says, so much as he was challenging and cruel. She felt humiliated, and her father started acting crazy, yelling, badgering her to eat. Of course, she now realizes that he was reacting out of fear. When they finally looked past the baggy clothes and the "slight" weight loss of a teenage vegetarian without much of an appetite, her folks really started to worry, and their worry translated into action. Almost immediately, they dragged Sarah to her pediatrician, who diagnosed her as anorexic. Naturally, Sarah denied that she had the kind of problem that could be reduced to a name—especially to *this* name. (Indeed, most patients reject their diagnosis and refuse treatment, particularly early on.) In Sarah's case, she was offended by the term. "I wasn't one of those prissy girls, desperate to be thin," she says. "I just said, 'Leave me alone,' and hoped that the whole thing would go away. The questions. The uncertainties. The doctors. Everything."

But there was no pushing the problem aside. Sarah started going to a therapist and a dietitian at her parents' insistence. The dietitian didn't do much good, because Sarah simply refused to follow her diet of prepared foods, and her parents weren't around enough to monitor what she was eating, but the therapist began to get through. Sarah felt a connection to this woman, seeing her as someone she could talk to and vent to. Her parents didn't really understand what was happening to her, her father most of all. Of course, how could she expect her parents to understand when she wasn't too clear on it herself? Her father, though, had a hard time with Sarah's strange eating habits. One night, for example, Sarah had locked herself in her room upstairs, ignoring her parents' calls to come down for dinner, choosing instead to eat a single graham cracker and be by herself. When she refused to join them at the table, her father came up and knocked the door down. Right off the hinges.

Soon, Sarah started seeing a new therapist, and this one recommended that Sarah be admitted to the Cleveland Clinic, one of the area's leading hospitals, even though there was no special program of treatment for Sarah's problem. There were, in 1995, a number of prominent clinics and hospitals specializing in the treatment of eating disorders, and there are even more today, but Sarah's parents and therapist figured that a big-city hospitalization was the only kind of emergency intervention available to them. Sarah was 14 years old, and her body weight had dropped to

60 pounds. It was becoming increasingly diffi-cult for her body to keep doing its job. She looked frail and emaciated. Her father, who Sarah says came up short in the bedside-manner department before he started to join her in therapy, told Sarah that she looked like a con-centration camp survivor. Her blood pressure was dangerously low; her pulse was weak, and her potassium levels were down; there was virtually no tissue around her organs, and her doctor worried that she wouldn't be able to start high school that fall.

What gets me here is what happened next. For all the well-meaning input provided by the doctor in charge of Sarah's case, and for all the better-late-than-never proactive moves put in place by her parents, Sarah was somehow assigned to the psychiatric ward at the Cleveland Clinic. The other kids on the ward had all kinds of emotional problems, but there wasn't an anorexic among them. The first meal they wheeled out for Sarah's consumption was a cheeseburger and some French fries. Sarah took one look at her plate and thought, *These people have got to be kidding!*

"That was truly the most terrifying day of my life," she describes. "The day I went into the hospital. I was screaming, crying like a baby, hanging on to my parents' legs to keep them from leaving me there. I'd been upstairs in my room, the door was closed, and my father just walked in and announced we were leaving. He didn't say where we were going. My mother started opening my drawers and taking out clothes and packing. I was like, *Oh, my God, what's going on?* But then I figured out what they were up to, and I calmed down a bit. Why? Well, I didn't think they'd go through with it. I thought it was some kind of bluff. They'd drive me down to the hospital, tell me they had no choice, and at the last minute I'd find some way to talk my way out of it. Anorexics are very manipulative. We manipulate, or we're into denial, and I was convinced we'd turn around and head right home. Right up until the time we pulled up to the curb and they sat me in a wheel-chair, I thought I was going home."

She wound up staying on the psych ward for a full week, under the 24-hour watch of a team of nurses. The first couple days in the hospital, she actually lost weight, down to a mere 59 pounds. The nurses wouldn't even let her write with a pad and pencil, that's how concerned they were about Sarah burning calories. If a nurse saw Sarah fidgeting in bed, they'd tell her to quit moving so she could conserve her energy. They wanted her to put on some weight fast, and they wanted to make sure it stayed on. They were constantly weighing her, drawing blood, and recalibrating her diet. She didn't realize it at the time, but she could have died. Between 5 and 20 percent of anorexics die of medical complications related to the illness, such as kidney failure or an erratic heartbeat. Food is the fuel we need to keep our bodies going, and without it, we eventually shut down.

After one week on the ward, Sarah was switched to a private room on the general in-patient care floor. Her food intake was still closely monitored by nurses. They wanted her to take in 2,200 calories each day, which was a huge jump from the couple hundred calories she'd been allowing herself. But she ate. She ate because she wanted to get out of there. Wanting to get well would come later. For now, she just wanted out. The nurses would dole out privileges based on Sarah's appetite. If she cleaned her plate, her parents could visit. If she cleaned her plate for a couple meals in a row, they'd let her watch a few innings of the Indians game. Otherwise, there were no visitors and no television. She wasn't allowed to shower, walk on her own power, or go to the bathroom by herself. The doctor in charge believed that she might also be bulimic, and if left alone she might stick a finger down her throat and undo all the good work she'd done in trying to eat.

"I kept telling them I wasn't bulimic," she reports. "They had my history. They'd spoken with my therapist. They just didn't understand."

After two frustrating, difficult weeks in the hospital, Sarah was finally sent home, although even she now admits that she probably wasn't ready to be out from under such close super-vision. But her insurance plan would only allow a two-week stay, and at the time, Sarah was only too happy to get out of there. She'd put back on some of the weight and was up to about 65 pounds, and if her condition was no longer life-threatening, it was still a cause for great concern. The biggest problem was this: She wasn't cured, not by a long shot. She'd managed to eat, because she'd been *forced* to eat, but without 24-hour monitoring and constant input from a dietitian, Sarah's parents worried that she'd slip back into her old habits.

Sarah, though, had another plan. She wasn't about to let herself be admitted into that hospital again, so she set about on a more determined course. If her doctor had her on a 1,200-calorie regimen, she made sure to eat at least 600 calories. It wasn't everything, but it was a whole lot better than she'd been able to manage just a few weeks before.

"To me, it was a big deal, the foods I was able to eat after I got out of the hospital," Sarah recalls. "To everyone else, it wasn't enough. I'd reverted back to some of my ways from before, like reading all the labels at the supermarket, and my parents were discouraged by this, but I was eating stuff I'd never eaten before I went into the hospital. I was making a real effort, and I was making real progress, but the weight gain wasn't really noticeable. Those first pounds, the fat went around my organs where I needed it. But you couldn't tell from just looking at me."

By the fall of her freshman year in high school, Sarah was ready to resume her normal routines. She got it in her head that the path to wellness lay in exercise, and she set out a training schedule that she felt would return her to health. The trouble was, her therapist didn't see that strenuous exercise matched Sarah's anorexic frame. (You have to realize, they wouldn't even let Sarah on a roller coaster, that's how worried they were over her frailty; her heart was so weak the excitement could have killed her.) Sarah was told that if she reached her target weight of 68 pounds, she would be allowed to walk 20 minutes each day. It wasn't exactly the kind of exercise Sarah was looking for, but she looked forward to those 20 minutes after she achieved her goal. And Sarah being Sarah, it wasn't long before she started abusing those privileges and stretching those walks to a half-hour, then 45 minutes, and then an hour.

"Almost as soon as I got out of the hospital, I became obsessive about exercise," Sarah says. "It's like I traded one obsession for another, but I thought this one would be a positive one. I didn't have a lot of friends anymore. I didn't go out at night or on the weekends. All I had, really, was this obsession about exercise. I had it all worked out in my head. I'd go from walking to running, to jumping rope, to maybe lifting some weights. As soon as I had my doctor's go-ahead to increase my workout, I pushed myself a little further. The goal, really, was to start playing softball again."

And she did. She wasn't the offensive force she'd been at her fighting weight, and she didn't get the kind of playing time she was used to, but Sarah made the team. She was a part of something. She was getting better, hanging out with kids her own age, renewing old friendships. She'd pushed her weight back up to 70 pounds, and she started working out at a nearby gym for women.

In her sophomore year, though, there were a few setbacks. Sarah's parents separated, and her boyfriend moved to North Carolina. Her dog—Sarah's one true companion for as long as she could remember—had to be put to sleep. She moved with her mom from the house she grew up in into a small, two-bedroom house in a neighboring town. "The thing with me," she says, "is that whenever I had a downfall, it affected me through eating. Or not eating. Things had been going so well for me, and then I was moved away from my few friends, my parents were divorcing, and next thing I knew, my weight was back down."

In her junior year, Sarah was over-the-top into her fitness thing—up at 4:30 every morning, jumping rope and lifting weights, and working out maybe six hours a day. Here again, she wasn't eating enough to support this kind of strenuous exercise, and she was still too skinny to make a real contribution on the softball team, but she felt healthy and strong. She looked, she says, like a marathon runner: lean, muscular, and wiry. Underneath that tiny frame, though, there was still a tense uncertainty over what to eat, and when, and for what reasons. She talked about her weight constantly. Or, to be accurate, her weight was talked about constantly—by her parents, her therapist, and her friends. She'd be in a stall in the girls' bathroom at school, and no one would know she was there, and she'd hear other kids talking about how skinny she was. "Oh my God, have you seen Sarah?" they'd ask each other.

Or her parents would bug her with questions about what she'd eaten for lunch or dinner. She'd gotten to where she was eating things like steamed vegetables and rice with a tall glass of milk for lunch, or a baked potato and a salad for dinner, and still she had to discuss every meal.

Finally, during her senior year, Sarah turned a corner—and, just as important, she took everyone who cared about her around that same corner with her. It started with the cross-country coach at school, who took one look at Sarah's lean frame and encouraged her to go out for the team. She'd never been particularly fast, but she was strong, and it seemed to be a good thing to do, a good place to direct her energies and her focus. Still, her parents weren't too wild about the idea of her running. Of all the activities she could have chosen, why that? And her therapist was also opposed to it, but Sarah was determined. Against their objections, she went out to a practice and competed in a five-mile timed trial—and came in second! She held back for most of the race and just dusted everybody at the end! Man, was she pumped, and feeling so positive about herself! She hadn't been *good* at something since she was 13, batting cleanup on the softball team. She started making all kinds of arguments in her head for why she should be allowed to run cross-country. It made her happy. She was making a bunch of new friends. Plus, if she had to run, she'd have to eat more. She'd find ways to keep the weight on because she needed the weight to do well.

Finally, her therapist caved in and granted Sarah permission to compete, as long as her pulse rate stayed above 60. Below that, the doctor felt, Sarah would be putting herself at risk. That was her comfort zone.

Sure enough, the first cross-country meet came around on the calendar, and at the last minute it occurred to someone in the school's administrative office that Sarah had not yet been cleared to run. She was on the bus with the rest of her team, all dressed and ready to head out to the meet, and the next thing she knew, the principal was on the bus, talking to the coach, and calling for Sarah to join them. They all stepped off the bus so the principal could take Sarah's pulse, and it came in at 59—one beat slower than her doctor's threshold, so she couldn't run.

"You can't imagine how upset I was," she recalls. "And it wasn't like it was some trained medical professional taking my pulse. It was the school principal!"

By the next meet, Sarah was cleared to run, and she finished fourth in the 5K in a field of 204 runners. She ended up qualifying for the state meet, the only person in her school to do so, and she got her picture in the paper. She took the clipping to her therapist "to prove myself," she says. "To show them I could do this. My parents, my doctor. They'd been holding me back and holding me back, telling me to be careful, but I needed to show them."

And show them she did.

At her senior prom, Sarah looked around at all the other girls in their dresses and how they filled them out, and she caught a picture of herself in a mirror and thought, *What's happened to me?* Everything came into perspective on this one night—the contrast between the life she'd lived during the past four years, and the lives enjoyed by her peers all through high school. "It was like I'd wasted all that time," she says. "I never went to any parties. I never did any of the things normal kids did. I just stayed in my room, worked out, or worried about food. And for what? This was supposed to be the best time of my life, and now it was over. I'd missed out on so much! It was like a knife to my heart. And all because of this strange obsession over food!"

Right then and there, Sarah decided to do something to deliver her illness one final blow—to knock it from her life forever. She turned to her date for the evening, a boy from another school she had met at one of her cross-country meets, and she asked him to take her out for an ice cream cone. She hadn't had one since her illness, and now the thought of one loomed as a kind of cure.

"I don't mean to simplify things and say that it was that one ice cream cone that did it," she says. "It didn't happen in just one day. But I went home with that ice cream cone that night, walked in the door, and my mother took one look at me and went, 'Oh my God!' She couldn't believe it. Truly, it was the beginning of the end. The obsession was gone."

Sarah's one of the lucky ones, and she recognizes that. "When you hit rock bottom, you finally see the disease for what it is," she explains. "People who are suffering with it need to know that there's hope. They're not going to have this sickness forever. Doctors used to tell me that I might never fully recover from it, but they were wrong. All it took, in my case, was self-realization. Knowing the problem, tackling the problem, and getting past it. I never went on any medication. What worked for me was developing my own self-esteem and confidence. I saw everyone else living a happy, carefree life, and that's what I wanted for myself. Thankfully, I had the willpower to do it."

❉ ❉ ❉

Sarah thriving today at 125 pounds.

Sarah at 68 pounds
(high school dance, freshman year).

Sarah's up for the challenge.

Sarah fights for health
and awareness.

"I wouldn't take back what happened to me."

CHAPTER FIVE

A Hole in the Earth

Sometimes I sit by myself in my office or my dressing room after a show, and I cry over the lives that are paraded in front of me—the hard choices people are forced to make, the hard roads they're forced to travel, the hard hands they've been dealt. And that's just on a typical day. It's the atypical days that really floor me, and the first time I heard about the ordeal of my friend Wesley Jordan, I was just knocked out, because what this young man was made to endure was so far off the map of human experience that it's a wonder he found his way to the other side.

To hear Wesley tell it, his was an unexceptional childhood. Up to a point. He grew up in the hills of Kentucky. His folks split when he was about nine, and after that he lived with his mother and his younger sisters, Sabrina and Montana. By the age of 13, they found themselves living with his mother's new husband, an itinerant gadfly who had tried his hand at a number of unsuccessful businesses and had even run for Congress in 1992. The guy's name was Steve Maynard, and he'd never amounted to much, and for some inexplicable reason, he would come to look upon Wesley as the primary reason for his professional failures. The family was living in the back of Maynard's vacuum sales and service store, in a storage space converted into an apartment, about a stone's throw from the Martin County courthouse, and yet despite his grim domestic situation, Wesley was doing okay in school. He pulled good grades. He had friends. He minded his mother and his sisters. He didn't figure that he'd be living in this small mountain town in back of a storefront forever.

Gradually, Maynard's demeanor toward his stepson, Wesley, began to shift from a kind of benign tolerance to all-out contempt, and the shift seemed to coincide with downturns in his various businesses. It's human nature, I suppose, to point a finger at someone else when things go wrong, but here, it started to follow an inhuman path, to the point where it was more than just pointing fingers. Wesley would pick up on things, in whispered asides and not-so-hushed conversations between Maynard and his mother, Bonnie. When the two adults argued, Wesley would hear that it was somehow his fault. Whatever tension there was between husband and wife, Maynard blamed Wesley for it. If another of Maynard's business ventures soured, he'd find a way to pin it on Wesley. The man's latest scheme was to publish his own newspaper, which basically consisted of articles clipped from established publications, but this, too, went nowhere. He put the publication together in a corner of his vacuum cleaner store and couldn't understand why no one was interested. The only explanation that made any sense, to this guy's warped way of thinking, was to blame it on his wife's kid.

Whatever it was, it fell on Wesley.

Soon enough, all of this laying of blame took on a physical dimension. One afternoon when Wesley was out helping his stepfather on an errand, Maynard reached into the back seat of his van where Wesley was sitting and bloodied his nose. He followed up his sucker-punch with a warning to Wesley not to tell his mother about it, because of course he'd come up with a story to discredit him, and it was already established in the family that Wesley was the screw-up, the one not to be believed, the one to be blamed for all their misfortunes, which at this point were mounting. So, Wesley took the beating like he had it coming, and he kept his mouth shut about it. He was raised to be respectful of his elders, and apparently that upbringing extended to folks who were in no way deserving of that respect. Plus, Maynard told Wesley he was connected to the Mafia, and he threatened the boy with far worse if he was foolish enough to open his mouth.

"I didn't really know what to do about it, to tell you the truth," Wesley says now, out from under his devastating past. "I didn't want anybody to know about it. I guess I thought maybe it was me, maybe I'd done something wrong, like Steve had said. And anyway, Mom seemed happy. The girls seemed all right. I didn't want to ruin all that, but then again, I started thinking, *This shouldn't be. It's not right. I didn't do anything. This is getting crazy.* I thought that maybe I should just get away somehow, go someplace else, but then I worried that if I did and he caught me, who knew what would happen?"

Other beatings followed. Although Maynard was trained as an emergency medical technician (EMT), it didn't seem like he cared a bit about another person's well-being. He smacked Wesley around, made him work in the hot Kentucky sun without water, or forced him to drink bleach and ammonia to induce vomiting if he thought the kid had eaten one of his candy bars. In fact, the only time he brought his EMT training to bear was when he tried to cover up the scars and bruises he left behind.

"He was always telling me I was plotting against him," Wesley says now, "or telling me I was trying to ruin things for him. One time, he said I was evil. Things weren't going well to begin with, but sure enough, I would get blamed for it, and every time I got blamed, I got hit for it as well."

The abuse came to a head one afternoon when Wesley was 14 years old. Maynard bound him with a length of bicycle chain, wrapped it around tight like a mummy, lifted Wesley up in a cradle position, and dropped him onto the hard floor. Over and over. Wesley refused to scream. He didn't want to give Maynard the satisfaction, or the ammunition to keep going. As it was, he was certain he'd broken a couple ribs, but they would have to heal on their own, along with the other scars and bruises. Maynard might cover them up, but he wouldn't administer any first aid. Wesley's mother was also a trained EMT, but she looked the other way, and when Maynard started chaining Wesley to the bathroom toilet or hot water heater, declaring him unfit to be with the rest of the family, she didn't make a move to help her son. His sisters didn't act out on their brother's behalf either, although they were so young it seems likely that they were deathly afraid they'd be in for some of the same if they spoke up.

For weeks at a time, Wesley would be chained to the concrete bathroom floor. It was the only bathroom in the building, which consisted of the storefront and the jerry-rigged apartment out back, and when his mother or sisters had to use the toilet, they were told to throw a towel over Wesley's head for privacy. When Maynard needed to do his business, he'd bark at Wesley that his sorry circumstance was his own doing. "He was always saying things like, 'See what you've done to yourself?'" Wesley recalls. "That was the only conversation there was. My mom, my sisters, they didn't say anything to me, and I didn't say anything to them. I kept quiet. I was afraid if I said anything, he'd think it was smart, and I'd be in for much worse."

Wesley's confinement in the family bathroom lasted for about 18 months. A year and a half!

I heard bits and pieces of Wesley's sad story in my office one afternoon, and right away I figured that we were talking about a couple hours, a day or two maybe, but this child was locked up day after day after day! During that time, Wesley was chained to the base of the toilet or the hot water heater, or even bound around the neck by a U-shaped Kryptonite bicycle lock to a wooden beam Maynard installed for just this purpose.

This last was about the worst, because Wesley couldn't sit down without hanging himself. And even though he was locked in the bathroom, he wasn't allowed to use the toilet. Most times, depending on how he was tied, there wasn't enough length of chain or rope to allow Wesley to use the toilet anyway, but he was instructed to relieve himself wherever he stood or lay. Every couple of weeks, someone would throw in a bucket and he would clean himself up, which usually happened when Maynard couldn't stand the stench anymore. And every week or two, if Wesley was lucky, he'd be let out to do some chore or other, or to tan himself in the sun to cover up some of the abuse marks that by now decorated his entire body. But his baseline existence, for 73 weeks, was the inside of a rundown storefront bathroom, with cracked fixtures and just enough light creeping through the rot in the walls to allow Wesley to make out night and day, and just enough air to let him guess at the change in seasons.

The newspaper accounts that came out of Kentucky when this story hit were enough to get you to question our place on this earth, but there was so much more to this terrible story that was never made public. The Associated Press reported that Wesley's mother and his two sisters would sometimes smuggle in table scraps for Wesley to eat on their regular trips to the bathroom, but Wesley later told me that this wasn't true. Once a week, or whenever he felt like it, Maynard brought him a bowl of slop—whatever was rotting or spoiling and about to be thrown out anyway—and Wesley would force himself to eat it because he knew there'd be nothing else. For a while, while the bathroom sink worked, there was running water, and when Wesley was able to reach the faucet, he could keep himself from becoming dehydrated, but when the sink broke and Maynard didn't move to fix it, Wesley was left dry. There was still running water in the toilet, but no matter how bad things got, Wesley told himself he wouldn't drink from it. No one would know, but he didn't want to give Steve Maynard the satisfaction just the same.

Realize, it wasn't just the indignity Wesley was made to endure, or the nearly solitary confinement, or the starvation. There were also ongoing beatings, chain whippings, and other violations. Broken fingers and ribs. A repeatedly broken nose. Maynard would open the door, use the toilet, and give Wesley a good hard kicking, the way a different sort of animal might kick a dog. Once, Maynard instructed his wife to hold Wesley down while he inserted a pair of pliers into the boy's anus, telling him that this was the sort of treatment he could expect when he went to jail. He'd pepper his beatings with all kinds of warnings, reminding Wesley that he was a good friend of the sheriff across the way, based in the county courthouse which Wesley could have seen if he'd been allowed to peer through one of the grimy windows in the crummy apartment. He had the poor boy brainwashed to think that if he made a move to save himself, he'd be in for far worse at the hands of the law.

Naturally, school officials came calling when Wesley didn't show up to begin ninth grade, but his mother petitioned the Board of Education to allow her to home-school all three of her children, and that seemed to quiet the authorities. The home schooling, of course, was a cruel joke. Wesley was locked in the bathroom, and his sisters spent their days in front of the television, but the folks in town pretty much left Bonnie and Steve Maynard alone after that.

If one of Wesley's friends came calling, or if someone asked about him in church, Wesley's mom and his sisters were told to tell people he'd gone to stay with relatives in another county. Folks bought the story without questioning it. It wasn't all that far-fetched, in Inez, Kentucky, for families to splinter apart like that without a word, and after a while, the friends stopped calling, folks stopped asking, and the inquiries died down. Wesley remembers feeling like he'd dropped through some kind of hole in the earth. Those were his words: *a hole in the earth*, and there wasn't a soul in the world who appeared to care for this 14-year-old boy. Not his mother. Not his sisters. Not his friends. Not his teachers. His biological father came calling a time or two, but the girls were hushed when he knocked on the door, the television turned down low, and eventually he gave up, too.

One of the incredibly bizarre pieces to this incredibly tragic story was that Steve Maynard actually filed for a second run for Congress in 1994, right in the middle of the cruel and unusual punishment he was dishing out on Wesley. Think about it: The guy was out campaigning and giving interviews and moving about like a respectable candidate, while at the same time he kept his wife's son chained to his toilet at home. In 1995, with poor Wesley still tied up in the bathroom, he ran for governor. I just couldn't get over this when I heard about it. Even after Wesley had managed to escape this man's craziness, Maynard thought to run *again* for Congress, this time in 1996 from his prison cell, where he was serving 20 years for seven counts of assault and one count of unlawful imprisonment.

So, yeah, Wesley Jordan did eventually escape the sick mistreatment meted out by his stepfather, and I don't mean to get ahead of myself in the story, but I do want to paint an accurate picture of what this guy must have been like—to have twice sought public office while torturing this young boy, and to have continued to move about in his community as if he was worth a damn.

Here's how Wesley finally managed to set himself free. It was raining late one morning.

Hard. Almost like it was hailing, but not quite. Maynard and Bonnie Jordan were having one of their usual drag-outs in the back room behind the store, and from what Wesley could make out, it was once again about him. Everything would be all right, Maynard hollered to his wife, if it weren't for *him*. This or that misfortune could have been avoided if it weren't for *him*. We wouldn't have to worry so much about the girls if it weren't for *him*. We wouldn't argue so much if it weren't for *him*. Whatever it was, it fell on Wesley, same as it ever was, only this time it was different. This time, Wesley had reached the low point in his young life where he didn't care anymore. Where he'd had enough. Where it didn't matter if he ran and Maynard caught him and dished it out ten times worse.

Just then, Maynard flung open the bathroom door and told Wesley they were going somewhere. He had to go into town, and he needed Wesley to run a couple errands for him so he could stay dry in the vehicle. Maynard threw a poncho at Wesley. "Here you go, you idiot," he barked at Wesley. "Throw that on."

(Strange—isn't it?—the way a man can leave a boy to live in such squalor, within an inch of his life and dignity, and still think to toss him a slicker to keep him dry in the pouring rain.)

As soon as they got outside, Maynard told Wesley he'd forgotten something in the back room. He told him to wait right there, or else, and he disappeared inside the store. Wesley thought to himself, *This is it. If you're gonna do it, then let's do it now and get it over with. If he catches up to me, he just does, and there's nothing I can do about that, but I can't take any more of this.* It didn't matter what the *or else* looked like.

And so Wesley Jordan took off, as fast as he could, down the same streets he used to walk a hundred times in a week, back and forth to school or to his friends' homes—the streets he hadn't seen at all in well over a year. He didn't think to run into the county courthouse, where the sheriff's office was situated, because he'd been told the sheriff was a friend of Maynard's and would probably throw Wesley in jail, so he went instead to a friend's house just down the road. But when he knocked on the door, a stranger answered. Wesley's friend had moved some months earlier, and he couldn't see asking someone he didn't know to help him out at a time like this, so he backed away from the front door and kept moving. At this point, he'd only gone a couple hundred yards from the store, so it wasn't like all that much time had passed since Maynard had gone inside for whatever it was he'd forgotten, and Wesley was kind of hoping he might not have noticed yet that he was gone. His next thought was to head out to another friend's house, only this friend lived about six miles away, and he didn't want to risk being out on the road long enough for Maynard to come looking for him, so he said a prayer.

"I saw a car coming," he recalls, "and I knew that it would either be Steve coming to pick me up and give it to me once and for all, or else it would a ride coming to take me where I was going. So I stuck out my thumb, hoping it would give me some luck, and sure enough, it did. It was a couple of older folks, kind enough to pick me up, and I was dripping wet, but it sure was nice of them."

He knocked on the door of a couple brothers he used to play basketball with. The parents were actually friends of Steve Maynard's, but they'd had a falling out and were no longer speaking. After all that time under his rule, Maynard had Wesley thinking he had friends all over town, but he didn't think these good people would turn him in. They knew Steve for what he was. As it turned out, they almost didn't recognize Wesley. He'd lost about 50 pounds during his confinement, and the first thing he did, once he made himself known, was to ask for something to eat. These good people fixed him a sandwich, got him into some warm clothes, and then they fixed him another sandwich. While he was wolfing down his food, Wesley dropped something on the floor and reached down to pick it up, and as he was doing so, the boys' father could see some of the marks and gashes left behind by Maynard's chains, imprinted on Wesley's arm.

"Steve had always told me to say I'd been in a motorcycle wreck," Wesley recounts, "and thrown into a barbed wire fence. He'd coached me on it, and I found myself telling this story to these nice people. I wasn't doing it to protect Steve, I don't think, so much as I was trying to save myself. I just wanted to get away, and I didn't care where I went to just as long as it was miles away from Martin County. I thought maybe I could get a little farther down the road that night, and I didn't want anyone else knowing what was going on."

But there was no fooling the guy who'd taken Wesley in. His name was Jed Smith, and he could tell straight off that those marks hadn't been made in a motorcycle wreck. He asked Wesley to lift his shirtsleeve, told him that it appeared he'd been tied up somehow, and then he took him aside and offered to help. "You don't have to tell me what happened," he said, "but if you're in any kind of trouble, we're here for you. We can't hide you out here, but I'll take you anywhere you need to go, call anyone you need me to call. But you've got to tell me something."

So, Wesley told them something. It was likely more than they were expecting to hear, but Jed Smith was good to his word. He shed a tear over what he saw, and his wife, Debbie, shed a few more, and finally Wesley agreed to let them go ahead and call the state troopers, to put an end to his particular hell. A warrant was issued for Steve Maynard's arrest that very night, and soon after that, Wesley's mom was arrested for her role in Wesley's unlawful imprisonment and torture. Wesley and his sisters were placed in foster care, and then with relatives, and within a few months, their biological father was awarded custody.

In the end, Bonnie Maynard served two years of her five-year sentence, and Steve Maynard was given twenty years, the maximum penalty in the state of Kentucky for a crime of this kind.

The judge in the case took Wesley aside after the sentencing and apologized for not being able to put his stepfather away for a longer period of time.

"The community let you down," he told Wesley during the hearing. "Your school, your teachers, and others. There is nothing I can say to make it right, but it's time to tell you that we care about you."

And that's about where Wesley and I got together, when the time had come for the rest of the world to deliver that same message. He was with his dad when we first spoke, and doing okay, but of course, how can you ever be doing okay after an ordeal like that? In Wesley's case, though, he was doing his best to put those black months behind him, and to look ahead to better days. In fact, his impulse to come on the show, hard as it was for him to speak about what had happened on such a public stage, was an important part of the healing process. The way Wesley saw it, in sharing his story, he was helping hundreds of victims trapped in similar situations all across the country; and in helping them, he was also helping himself.

Yes, that's correct—there are hundreds of victims trapped in similar situations all across the country! As a matter of fact, my friend Dave Pelzer chronicled the "singled out" scenario in his memoir *A Child Called It.*

I should mention here that the aftermath to Wesley's story hasn't all been positive. He no longer speaks to his sisters—or, more accurately, they no longer speak to him. They're pretty upset with Wesley for turning in his mother, the way he had to, and Wesley figures that's just something they'll have to learn to deal with. They're still young, and they'll either come to terms with it someday, or they won't. And he's got no relationship with his mother now that she's served her sentence. There's no forgiving the way she let him down and looked the other way.

I'd be remiss if I didn't give Wesley the credit for inspiring me to write this book. The idea first came to me after Wesley had reappeared on the show to update the thousands of fans who kept him in their hearts. A childhood friend of Wesley's had seen him on the show and remembered him and his disappearance from school. She wrote to me to express that his strength had given her the courage to persevere through a family tragedy. She wanted to thank him. We thought it would be nice to surprise him with the thank you on air. A short time after we taped that show, my producer came to me with the news that Wesley and the young lady had gotten engaged. He was in a private school, trying to catch up on all the schooling he'd missed during his imprisonment, and things were really looking up for him. There it was, the epitome of hope and courage. And the idea behind *A Dozen Ways to Sunday* was born.

However, as in most real-life stories, happily ever after isn't that easy. Another tragedy came along, and this one cost Wesley his beloved aunt—and the chance at the lifetime of happiness he had so clearly pictured in his head. His aunt and his fiancée were in a terrible car crash, and his aunt was killed instantly. Wesley's fiancée survived, but things were never right between them after that.

"Something was missing," he tries to explain. "Can't say what it was. I don't think we knew what it was. But we couldn't work it out. Everything changed."

What hasn't changed is Wesley's desire to find the girl of his dreams and start a family. "That's all I ever wanted," he says. "Even back then, locked in the bathroom, I'd think about it. It was never about money, or being on top. Those kinds of things just don't count for me. I'm just into the basic things in life. A family. A little house of my own. A good job. Simple things. That's all I really want."

Is he worried about bringing a child into a world that could shower on a small boy the same kind of violence, neglect, and cruelty he was made to suffer?

"Not at all," he says. "I believe we all have our ups and downs in life, and we just have to learn how to take our little bits of each and go with it. There's no defending what Steve did to me, and when I think about it, it just boils through me. Picking on a kid four times smaller than you? There's no explaining it. But I always knew, deep down, that I'd see it through. God would see me through. I prayed, back there in that bathroom. Many times. I'd beg God to get me out of there, and I believe He did. Ultimately, He had a hand. It wasn't all me. If it weren't for Him, I wouldn't be here."

Wesley, as of this writing, is living in an apartment in New Jersey with three of his closest friends from back home in Kentucky, working a good job in window construction, and putting away some money so he can go to college someday. Wesley never did finish high school, but he's got his GED in sight, and he's looking ahead without looking back.

"I wouldn't take back what happened to me," he allows. "People ask me all the time, if you could let anybody have your place, would you? And the answer is no. It brought me out a lot stronger. I have all these emotions I never knew I had, and I care deeply for things in a way I never did before. And I wouldn't want anybody else to go through what I had to go through. Not even Steve Maynard. I don't care who you are or what you've done, it shouldn't happen to you, what happened to me. But it made me a better person, a more caring person, a more respectful person."

And even though he won't say it, it made Wesley Jordan a more determined person—to push on, to go to college, and to get on with his life—that is, to make his burden a blessing.

❋ ❋ ❋

Wesley Jordan has started
a new life with his close
friends in New Jersey.

Today, Wesley reflects on the past but looks forward to the future.

Dr. Kelsey Caplinger stands in front of Camp Aldersgate, the entrance into the Med Camp grounds.

CHAPTER SIX

Fresh Air

*D*id you ever grab ahold of an idea and let it take you beyond your wildest imaginings? Or, did you ever set off down one path and find yourself headed toward a whole new goal? That's sort of what happened to Dr. Kelsey Caplinger, a pediatric allergist from Little Rock, Arkansas, who got it in his head to start a summer camp program for some of his asthma patients, and who looked up after his initial efforts to find that he'd created something far bigger than his dreams.

It was a simple notion at first—find a venue for a dozen or so asthmatic kids so that they might enjoy the well-documented benefits of a summer camp experience: communal living, exercise, outdoor pursuits, and the chance to blossom away from home in a new environment. The trouble was, there weren't enough acutely asthmatic patients in and around the Little Rock area to justify the launch of a full-fledged, full-summer program, so Dr. Caplinger tailored his idea to the specific needs of his patients and the specific demands of his community.

Instead of thinking big, he thought small. He wasn't out to reinvent the wheel on this one, so he visited a number of asthma camps, spent a week as camp doctor at a facility in West Virginia, and came away thinking that he could offer the same services (and a little something else, besides) right in his own backyard. Of course, if he only had enough campers to fill beds for a week or two, it made no sense to go looking for a dedicated camp property, so, instead, he looked around for some cabins, a mess hall, a lake, and a couple of ball fields that he could call his own on sort of a time-share basis.

Dr. Caplinger found exactly what he was looking for at Camp Aldersgate, a Methodist retreat just outside the city, located on 160 wooded acres that might as well have been in the middle of nowhere. But it was just a ten-minute drive from his home, and less than a mile from the largest community hospital in Arkansas, so it couldn't have been better situated. The camp had a long history of service to disadvantaged persons throughout the state, with a variety of programs tailored to everyone from seniors to school groups, church organizations to families, but no one had ever thought about housing a program there for *medically* disadvantaged children. Much of Camp Aldersgate's emphasis up to then was in reaching out to kids who couldn't otherwise afford a summer camp experience. The twist here would be reaching out to kids who didn't even think about looking for that same experience. Money was still important, the same as always, but it wasn't necessarily the issue.

"I went in to talk to the director," Dr. Caplinger recalls, "and I laid out my plan for him. I told him that I wanted to start the camp the following year if we could. He felt that this was a poor idea, and told me instead that we should do it *this* year. Right away, almost. That's how strongly he took to the idea. So we took our few cabins, filled them with about a dozen campers, and went to it."

Thirty-one years later, Dr. Caplinger's Med Camps of Arkansas boasts one of the largest and most comprehensive traditional residential camping programs for children with specific medical conditions and physical disabilities. It's the largest in the state, the largest in the country, and as far as anyone can tell, it's the largest in the world. Indeed, we couldn't find a comparable program anywhere, and what makes the Med Camps model so unique is the way that it makes room for so many children, with so many types of illnesses and disabilities, from so many backgrounds. The place is a regular melting pot of chronically ill and disabled young people, and I've got to tell you, I've never seen a more joyous collection of souls in any one setting—each out for nothing more than a good time and a firm footing.

To date, there have been more than 7,000 campers who have spent at least a part of one summer in the Med Camps program, and they run the gamut. There's a week set aside for kids with diabetes, a week for kids with cerebral palsy, a week for kids with spina bifida, and a week for kids with muscular dystrophy. Kids suffering from epilepsy, cancer, arthritis, and asthma also get their own sessions, and if a sponsoring health agency can make a case for any other group of afflicted children, Dr. Caplinger will see that they get a week of camp, too—all at no cost to the campers or their families. And all set against a traditional camping program that includes hiking, canoeing, swimming, music, arts and crafts, sports, climbing, and a Special Olympics to cap each session. Each session is designed to instill in each camper the kind of self-confidence that might not find them during the rest of the year.

The goals of the Med Camps program are clear:

- Provide a camping opportunity for medically disadvantaged children.

- Offer an opportunity for campers to live and work with others.

- Enable campers to develop a sense of independence with respect to their particular disease or disability.

- Encourage campers to manage their own day-to-day care.

- Create an environment where campers can establish friendships with other children in similar circumstances.

It really is a thing to see, on any given week during the summer, the way these kids move about the camp with a growing autonomy. The personal and interpersonal triumphs they record are awe-inspiring, as are the memories they make. And the smiles that bounce from one face to the next are contagious.

"One of our counselors here is fond of saying that there's a miracle a minute out here at camp," Dr. Caplinger notes, "but that's not our limit, that's our average."

The miracle, really, is that for a lot of these kids, camp has become their only place to shine, or to feel at home. (Actually, here's a better way to put it: It's their *first* place to shine or feel at home, because they take the emotional tools that have been sharpened at camp back into their daily routines.)

"Each one of these campers may be the only kid in their school district with their particular disease or their particular disability," Dr. Caplinger observes, "so who else can they talk to other than the kids at camp? There's no one else in a motorized wheelchair at their school. There's no one else who's also learned to administer his own insulin. There's no one going through what they're going through."

Depending on the sponsoring agency during each week of camp, there can be anywhere from 25 to 65 campers roaming the nature trails of Camp Aldersgate. The staff-to-camper ratio varies according to the medical and support needs of each group of campers. During cerebral palsy week, for example, Med Camps needs to recruit a full-time wheelchair pusher for almost every camper, so that puts a cap on the number of available beds. Diabetic campers require less hands-on care, so that program enrolls about twice as many kids.

Each session, no matter how many slots are available, is filled to capacity. It turns out that there aren't enough weeks in the summer to fill the need—and, regrettably, there are some kids who are turned away because Camp Aldersgate doesn't have the staff or the facilities to accommodate their extra-special needs.

"That's the toughest part of what we do," Dr. Caplinger allows. "To have to say no to a kid who wants to go to camp. We try to direct them to programs that are better suited for their illness or disability, and most times we're successful, but from time to time, we can't make a match, and it just breaks my heart."

Naturally, the Med Camps model didn't always enjoy such broad acceptance, and in the early going, Dr. Caplinger faced an against-the-current battle to get local health agencies to throw in with him. Parents, too, weren't exactly lining up for applications for their children. It was one thing to open a camp program for medically needy kids, but it was quite another to fill the bunks with campers. Dr. Caplinger could find the asthmatic kids through his own practice, but by the second season, it became apparent that the need reached far beyond his patients.

In that second summer, Dr. Caplinger offered

a second session for non-ambulatory patients, and that was a kind of makeshift affair. The cabins weren't properly fitted for wheelchairs, the doors to the bathrooms were too narrow, there weren't blacktop areas for ball playing, and there were no ramps or sidewalks. One hard rain and these poor kids were stuck in a thick of mud in their chairs. The motto for that summer was "Make do," and that's about what they managed, but Dr. Caplinger and company finished out the session with a bunch of new ideas for the summers ahead.

The real trouble, after retrofitting the cabins and grounds for wheelchairs and such, came in recruiting potential campers who might benefit from the program, and then in convincing parents and physicians to place their kids in Dr. Caplinger's care.

"I happened to be the chairman of the Arkansas chapter of the American Academy of Pediatrics (AAP) that year," Dr. Caplinger explains, "so it wasn't hard to get our first group in. We had that medical credibility. And then we reached out to the state medical society and got them involved because it was so terribly important to be able to tell the parents that this was something endorsed by their own doctors. It's so frightening to send a child off to a camp like this for the first time, especially a child with therapy requirements or other special needs, so we wanted to offer every conceivable assurance."

And yet even with all these assurances, the Med Camps program was still a hard sell. For his second season, Dr. Caplinger managed to convince the local Easter Seals chapter to offer a week of camp to children in their program, and from there, he set his sights on the Arkansas Arthritis Foundation.

"I was on the board," he explains. "I knew the people involved. That's how we worked it back in those early days as we tried to expand, and to reach as many children as possible. I just went through the phone book, went out to these different agencies, and told them what we were up to. Usually I'd know at least some of the folks on the boards of these agencies, so it's not like I was going in cold. I'd say, 'Would you like to have a camp?' And the comment was always the same: 'It's not in the budget.' To which I'd always say, 'Well, if we pay for it the first year, do you think it would be a good idea?' After that, they thought it was a good idea, and what would happen was, the following year, the agency would pick up some of the cost, and the year after that, they'd pick up a little more. We never worked on a contract basis, just a handshake. They paid what they could, as much as they could, and by the time they were paying their own way, we'd moved on to help some other group of kids."

It's important to emphasize that it wasn't enough to simply identify the kids in need throughout the state. There had to be the right number of comparably able kids, at the right age, who wanted to take advantage of the program. The parents had to want to send their children away, and the various illnesses and disabilities had to match up in such a way that programming or staffing wouldn't be a problem.

In the beginning, these pieces didn't always gel, so over time, Dr. Caplinger stumbled onto a three-pronged approach to keep the effort going, and it's the same approach they follow today. The folks at Camp Aldersgate provide the facility, the food, the counselors, insurance, maintenance . . . the nuts and bolts of the camping program. Med Camps, now a nonprofit project of the Arkansas AAP, offers medical support, equipment, donations, and supplemental funding for capital improvements and tuition; and the co-sponsoring agencies (United Cerebral Palsy of Central Arkansas, Arkansas Spinal Cord Commission, Arkansas Epilepsy Society, and so on) handle recruitment, special-needs staffing and training, and a fair share of tuition funds.

By 1985, the Med Camps project was such a tremendous hit with local doctors and health-care agencies that other folks couldn't help but notice. Doctors in other parts of the country traveled to Little Rock to gather ideas for their own versions of the same good idea, and Dr. Caplinger was awarded the prestigious President's Volunteer Action Award in a White House luncheon presided over by President Ronald Reagan.

Today, Med Camps has grown to where it's now the largest, longest-running program at Camp Aldersgate; in some weeks, depending on enrollment, it occupies the entire camp facility. Med Camps of Arkansas, Inc., has funneled more than $250,000 in donated funds into various improvement projects at the camp, including the installation of ramps, handicapped-accessible bathrooms, an indoor activity center, and a state-of-the-art swimming pool. The Methodist church that owns the property and sponsors the camp has come to regard the Med Camps effort as an essential part of its ministry—and the campers have come to regard their time in the woods as an essential part of their growing up, an annual chance to set aside what ails them. And somewhere in the middle, the hundreds of volunteers each summer look on their work as an essential aspect of their own lives and the way they see the world.

That's one of the unheralded aspects of Med Camp's success—the way it runs on volunteer fuel. Last summer, there were nearly 300 volunteers on board, in one way or another, logging more than 17,000 volunteer hours. Seventeen thousand! In past summers, that number has approached 25,000. Break it down and you'll see that this is about the equivalent of 13 full-time, nine-to-five, five-days-a-week volunteer positions.

Most of these hours were logged by hardworking professionals—many of them doctors, nurses, therapists, and other medical professionals who stand as the camp's foundation. Each week, just to give you an idea of how things work, there's a doctor on board specializing in whatever illness or disability has got the run of the place. Happily, Dr. Caplinger reports that there's never been a problem recruiting volunteer doctors. Due to the camp's location (just outside the city), it's possible for a doctor to be on-call, or keep office hours at his practice, and still be available to campers on a nearly full-time basis. The nurses, though, are on-site 24 hours a day, and what's remarkable here is that they have to take vacation days from their hospital and office jobs in order to fulfill their duties. And still, they come.

The counselors get paid, but it's not a whole lot of money, so it's essentially volunteer work as well. Maybe $150 for the entire summer, for a 10- or 11-week schedule. (A veteran counselor might earn $200 for the season.) It works out to maybe $.25 an hour, plus all the bug juice they can drink, so clearly they're there out of the goodness of their hearts. Some, it turns out, are there to sample the varied aspects of a career in medicine, and that's been one of the enormous side benefits to the Med Camps program.

"We had one fellow with us for a couple summers," Dr. Caplinger recalls. "His father was a doctor. His mother was a doctor. His brother was a doctor. I think his sister was a nurse. And this young man was resisting following down the trail. He didn't think medicine was for him, but somehow he wound up on our staff, and eventually he became our head counselor. Before any of us knew it, he was off at medical school. He decided medicine *was* for him, and he'll tell you that he reached that decision because of his time at camp. In fact, he even married another Med Camps counselor, and now they have a couple of kids and he's a pediatrician down in Texas.

"Every summer, it seems, there's a story like that—an example of how an experience at our camp helped one of our young people make a decision about their life or career. Sometimes that decision goes the other way, though. We had a young woman working with us, she thought she'd be a nurse, and after a summer changing bandages and catheterizing campers and handling seizures, she decided she didn't like that kind of work at all. Now she's an accountant, and grateful for the experience, so you never know how it's gonna go."

Spend some time talking to Kelsey Caplinger, and it won't surprise you at all that he's made such a selfless gesture with respect to his life's work. He's got a sweet, gentle disposition; a dry, down-home sense of humor; and a humble perspective that leaves you feeling that it's been a privilege for him to have made a difference in just this way. Truly, this good man doesn't get what the big deal is when folks start fussing about the program he's created and the lives he's changed. He doesn't even see that he had all that much to do with it, beyond getting it going in the first place. To Kelsey Caplinger, the Med Camps program is merely an extension of who he is and how he was raised.

"I feel really fortunate to have been able to do something a little bit different," he says, "but I always knew I'd be helping people in some way. I grew up in a small town in Arkansas, and my mother and father were always very active in the community. I felt that was the way you were supposed to be. It always amazed me when a colleague used his practice as an excuse to not do something. He was too busy for this, or too busy for that. Back when I was a boy, if somebody died or got sick, my mother was the first one there with the green beans. My dad was a small-town merchant, and he took his turn as president of the Chamber of Commerce. I always sold magazines and newspapers to raise money for different class projects and things, and it never occurred to me that everyone didn't do it."

As he considers retiring from his medical practice, Dr. Kelsey Caplinger looks ahead to spending more time on his Med Camps project. Or . . . not. For the past 20 or so years, he's been trying to bring in some younger doctors to work on the project on an ongoing basis, but so far he hasn't found anyone to share his vision of the big picture. His colleagues are too happy to pitch in with a week of donated services here, or a week there, but there's no one to go to all the meetings for him, to keep up with contributions, or work to improve the program and the facilities.

"I've gotten so much credit over the years for this thing," he says, "and surely I don't deserve it all, but people know me, or they know *of* me, because of this camp. And I'm always telling people that this camp is more than just me. In fact, during the summer, it runs just fine without me. I was the catalyst, I guess, but there are an enormous number of people who work on this thing. It's a big job, but a big job is just a series of small jobs; and many, many people are out there doing their small jobs every single day of the year. It's not fair that I get all the credit. A lot of the kids, at this point, don't even have any idea who I am. And I like that just fine. They know the director of the camp for the week they attend, someone from their sponsoring agency, but they don't know me.

"Why, just the other day, I was out at the camp with my cameras, trying to snap the perfect picture, to really capture what it means to be at camp. I had two cameras around my neck, one for color and one for black-and-white, and I was walking around, shooting away. The counselors all knew me, of course, and I had my friends all over, in the office and in the infirmary, but the kids had no idea. Finally, I was off by one of the fields, and one of the kids pointed me out to one of the counselors and asked, 'Hey, who's that old guy with the cameras?' I had to laugh when I heard that."

When, precisely, did Dr. Caplinger realize that he was onto something that would outpace his initial vision, something that might someday stand as his legacy? It was during one of his first summers at Camp Aldersgate, back when they were still offering a general medical week with a mixed bag of campers. There was one camper named Jimmy who was suffering from cystic fibrosis.

"This little boy was breathing with about 20 percent of his lung," the doctor recalls, "coughing up gobs of mucous if he ran about 15 yards, but he was out there, and active, and having a good time. At one point, on a trip to the infirmary, he watched as one of the nurses was teaching a diabetic camper how to give herself a shot. They were using an orange for practice, and little Jimmy watched, and a little while later he said, 'Gosh, I'm glad I don't have to do that every day.' He'd found someone worse off than he was, and for a while, he didn't have to feel so bad about his own situation. He died Christmas of that year, but he got a perspective on life he wouldn't have gotten otherwise. That's how I knew we were moving in the right direction."

These days, there are reminders every summer, and during the winter they ring forth in the countless cards and e-mails that come in from happy campers and grateful parents:

"Can I live here forever?"

"I'd rather stay here than go to Disney World."

"Camp rocks."

"I never shot a bow and arrow before. It was cool."

"It made me feel like I could conquer anything."

"I like camp because it's fun and I don't have to pick tomatoes."

I suppose there's a story that goes with this last statement—but then, there's a story to go with every last one of them. Seven thousand . . . and counting.

❁ ❁ ❁

"There's a miracle a minute out here at camp . . . but that's not our limit, that's our average."

A counselor and camper benefit from the lake at Med Camp.

Dr. Caplinger and two campers enjoy the afternoon.

"God is not gonna put any burden on my shoulders He knows I can't handle."

CHAPTER SEVEN

Persevere

I have enormous respect for courage and determination, which is why I think my interest was sparked when I heard the saga of Pleasure Heard, a University of Chicago sophomore who has lived through a kind of hell and has still been able to thrive.

Hers might have been a horrific story: As a young teenager, Pleasure was doused with alcohol and burned by a neighborhood gang member, yet she not only survived the attack, she also managed to retain her number-one class ranking throughout high school and see her attacker put away for 45 years. These were both amazing accomplishments—and for Pleasure, there was never any doubt in her mind that she would emerge on the winning end of the deal.

She had it tough enough. She never knew her father, and her mother bailed when Pleasure was about seven years old, leaving Pleasure and two older sisters, Precious and Princess, to bounce around in Chicago's foster-care system for the rest of their adolescence. (Yes, her mother had a gift for naming her children, but to hear Pleasure tell it, that was about it for the woman's parenting skills.) By Pleasure's count, she'd attended ten different grammar schools, and by the time she landed in high school, she was living in Englewood, one of the city's toughest neighborhoods, with one of the highest incidences of rape, murder, and gang violence in Chicago. About half the kids who started Englewood Technical Preparatory Academy with Pleasure freshman year didn't make it to graduation four years later.

"God is not gonna put any burden on my shoulders He knows I can't handle," Pleasure notes of her time in school and her situation at home.

And yet, He very nearly did.

For four years, she says, she's never been able to share the details of the time she was set on fire without breaking down in tears, but she was able to tell them to me and my producers with grace and strength. Here's what happened: Toward the end of her freshman year in high school, and throughout the following summer of 1997, Pleasure had met and befriended a gangbanger named Kevin Phelps, who had been confined to a wheelchair as a result of a gunshot wound in a gang-related shooting a year earlier.

"He knew my cousin," Pleasure recalls. "We started talking, and he seemed nice. He didn't have too many friends. The people he used to run with weren't with him anymore." Soon, Pleasure started visiting Phelps once or twice each week, shopping for groceries for him, fixing things around the house, and helping out in what ways she could.

"He was paralyzed," she explains. "There was a lot he couldn't do for himself, so I went by and helped him. I didn't really know too much about what had happened to him. I didn't really ask."

There was nothing even remotely romantic about her friendship with Phelps. "It wasn't at all like that," she explains. "He was much older than me. Why would I be interested in a man like that? Why would he be interested in a girl like me? No, it was just me going by in the afternoons keeping him company, running errands. I felt sympathy for him."

Summer rolled around, and Pleasure took a job at her school. For a stretch of three weeks or so, she couldn't find any time to visit Phelps. She kept meaning to, but the job was winding down, she was gearing up for sophomore year, and things were just too busy. And besides, it wasn't the kind of thing where they had a standing appointment; she just went when she could and figured she'd go again as soon as she could. That's how it is when you do a good turn, she thought. You fit it in where it makes sense, and you don't worry about it where it doesn't.

School started, and Pleasure joined the volleyball team. One afternoon after practice—September 7, 1997, to be precise—she crossed the street to catch the city bus home and noticed two guys hanging out of their car, calling out to her. Phelps used to call her "Nana," and no one else at her school knew her by that name, and here were these two guys calling her "Nana" and motioning for her to get her things and get in their car.

Pleasure didn't know these guys or recognize the vehicle; she was savvy enough not to like the look of this scene, so she kept walking to the bus, and she rode it to where she had to switch lines. When she got off, she noticed the same car, with the same two guys, still calling out to her. It was about five o'clock in the afternoon, a pretty busy time out on the streets, so she figured she'd be okay waiting the couple minutes for her transfer. But one of these guys sidled up to her and stuck a gun in her back and told her to get in the car. He grabbed her jacket and started pushing her around. No one around seemed to notice, or to care. There was nothing for Pleasure to do but get in the car.

"The whole ride, wherever we were going, nobody said anything," she remembers. "They didn't tell me who they were or where they were taking me. Just silence, the whole way there. We drove for maybe a couple of miles, and there was just quiet."

Naturally, Pleasure recognized the street and the building as they pulled up, just in front of Phelps's place, and now what she couldn't understand was why she had been summoned here in this way. He could have called if he'd needed to see her. It made no sense. Kevin was a friend of hers. His friends called him Sniper, but she called him Kevin, and she couldn't figure it out. She went from being afraid to confused, as the two guys led her into Phelps's room. He was sitting on the bed, his wheelchair off to the side. There was a huge cast on his arm, fingers to elbow. His friends left and shut the door behind them. The television was on in the background, and at this point it was about 5:30. Pleasure remembers noting the time based on what show was playing on TV.

"Where you been?" Phelps started asking. "Who you been with? Why you trying to get away from me?"

"He was acting crazy," Pleasure says. "Jealous. I don't even know what he was acting like. The whole time I'd known him, eight months, he'd never said these kinds of things, or acted this way. 'Where you been? Who you been with?' Over and over. I was just stunned. I asked him, 'What's wrong with you? Quit playing crazy.'

This just went on and on, and finally he looked at me and said, 'Take your clothes off.' This just threw me, because I didn't even like to go into a swimming pool with a guy, dressed in a bathing suit, and here he was, ordering me to take my clothes off. We were friends, but there was nothing going on between us. I looked at him like, 'What?' but he grabbed me by the shirt and pulled the biggest gun I'd ever seen out from underneath the bed, and he said it again: 'Take your clothes off.' So I started taking my clothes off. I knew he wasn't playing. I knew something was wrong. I left my socks on, and my bra and panties, but he waved the gun at me and said, 'Everything,' so I took those off, too. I left my socks on, though. And I stood there in front of him, naked, with just my socks on, wondering what he was gonna do next, what would happen."

Phelps told Pleasure to pull a chair over to his bed, and she did. He told her to sit down on it, and she did. She thought, *This man is crazy, and he has a gun, so I best do what I'm told*. Phelps sat with the gun on his lap, and then he reached down for another, and placed this second gun under his pillow. The whole time, the television was on, and now and then his attention would drift to whatever show he was watching, and then back to Pleasure. "Where you been?" he'd ask, again and again. "Who you been with?" Over and over.

Finally, at 6:30, the show *Martin* came on, and Phelps asked Pleasure to turn up the volume—all the way up, until she couldn't turn the knob anymore. "The television was, like, blasting," she says. "Kevin had to yell for me to hear him. It was the strangest thing. I was scared and naked, and there was this sitcom on in the background, and people were laughing and everything, and this man had a gun on me."

At one point during the show, Phelps asked Pleasure to fetch him a cup of water, so off she went, naked, in just her socks, and brought back an eight-ounce glass of cold water. Phelps said the glass wasn't big enough, so Pleasure went looking for a tumbler, wondering what he needed all that water for, and when she returned to the bed, she saw him pouring something into another cup. *Alcohol,* she thought, but it didn't really register. He was fidgeting, reached into his pocket for a lighter, but here again, Pleasure didn't really notice. It all happened fast, almost in the background. She saw it, but she didn't process it. She was well past the point where she was ready to do what she was told just to get out of there. Phelps told her to sit back down on the edge of the bed, and as she did so, he threw the cup of alcohol at her and immediately flicked his lighter. Before she could think about what was happening Pleasure was engulfed in flames.

"It was all in an instant," she says, "and I couldn't think. I was shocked. I didn't know what to do. To this day, I don't know why I didn't think to stop, drop, and roll. That's what they teach you in school, in a fire—to stop, drop and roll—and I knew that. I kept hearing the words in my head, but it didn't come. All I could think was to run. I was 15 years old, this man had a gun in my face, I was naked and on fire, and all I knew was to run. A part of me was thinking clearly, though. I'd never been through the whole house, but I knew there was only a half-bath downstairs, so I must have figured there'd be a full bath upstairs, because next thing I knew I was running up those stairs, I guess thinking that I could find a tub. There was a wheelchair at the top of the stairs, and I remember hassling with it, trying to get it out of my way, trying to get to the washroom, all the time not thinking to stop, drop, and roll.

"When I got to the washroom, the water didn't work. There was no pressure. And I thought, *Why doesn't the water work? What's going on that the water doesn't work?* There were just little sprinkles, and I must have struggled with that water for a couple minutes because that's how long it took to put the fire out, and the whole time I wasn't thinking about the pain I was in; I was just thinking about getting out of there. I was frantic. I thought about finding some clothes and jumping out the window, but it was a couple flights down and I thought I'd kill myself in the fall."

Somehow, Pleasure got it together enough to come back downstairs, to try to exit out the front door. Her flesh felt as if it were melting. To leave the house, she had to pass by the room where Phelps sat waiting, and as she did so, he called out to her. "Don't you start crying on me," he said. "You better not cry."

He pointed one of the guns at her as he said this, and she vowed not to cry, or to run. Then he motioned for her to approach him on the bed, where he'd set out a couple packs of iodine swabs, two to a pack, and a jar of Vaseline. He set down his gun and started rubbing the Vaseline over Pleasure's burns, and it was all she could do not to scream. The jelly trapped the heat in a weirdly excruciating way. It was like nothing she'd ever felt before. Then he started rubbing her with the iodine swabs. She wished she could move and bolt for the door, but she couldn't. Her skin was burning, bubbling up, and this strange, sick gangbanger was playing doctor on her burns. He held a gun in one hand and worked on her skin with another, and she couldn't tell if he was trying to help her or cause her more pain.

At one point, he reached for some peroxide, and poured some of this onto his mixture of Vaseline and iodine, and Pleasure could have sworn that her skin was dripping down her leg.

"It's like it wasn't even skin anymore," she recalls. "Like it was a coating that had been melted away."

The television was still blaring, and Phelps watched as he worked. At about 6:45, during a commercial, he turned to Pleasure and said, "If I don't kill you, what you gonna say happened to you?" All this stuff going on, Pleasure burned beyond recognition all over her legs, stomach, and pubic area—40 percent of her body, as it turned out!— and this guy was determined to watch the rest of his sitcom and come out of this thing without being implicated. There wasn't just a screw loose here, she thought; this guy was completely whacked!

"I couldn't think of anything to say that would have convinced him to let me leave the house the way that I was," she recalls. "I told him I'd say whatever he wanted. I told him to tell me what to say." He came up with a story that she was raped and burned on the way home from school by some boys she didn't know, and he worked out all the little details so that it made sense. As she dressed, he went over it with her to make sure she had it straight. As she put her clothes back on, she knew that they would stick to her body and that it would hurt something fierce to peel them back off, but she didn't care. She just wanted out, and this was what it would take to get out.

The whole way home, even waiting for the

bus, she wouldn't let herself cry. She'd made a promise to herself not to let this bastard make her cry, and she was holding to it. But when she finally reached home, where she was staying with her sisters, she couldn't hold back the tears.

"I started peeling off my clothes," she recalls, "and screaming and crying, the whole time saying, 'It's not for setting me on fire! It's not for setting me on fire!' He couldn't hear me, but I didn't want him to think he'd made me cry."

Her sisters called for an ambulance, and soon enough, the pain medications started to kick in. The doctors and nurses began packing her burns with wet towels, and soon after that, she went blank. She remembers talking to a police officer, who asked her for Phelps's name and address, but Pleasure doesn't remember anything after that. She remained in intensive care at the University of Chicago Hospital for two weeks, and as soon as she was able to think clearly, she started asking for her schoolbooks. She'd been number one in her class all freshman year, and she didn't want to get left behind at the beginning of sophomore year.

She had to undergo 16 hours of surgery and additional skin grafts, she had to relearn how to walk (she couldn't even bend her knee to walk up a flight of stairs!), she had to get used to this new picture of herself she carried around inside her head, and all she could really think about was her schoolwork.

"I knew I wasn't anything without my education," she says now. "One thing no one can ever take away from me is my education. This man took away my body, or my skin, but no one can take what I know away from me. And that's what I was thriving on."

To this day, the nurses on the burn unit at the hospital still talk about the young girl who reached for her schoolbooks as soon as she could, despite the lousy hand she'd been dealt. To be itching to study a day or two after suffering injuries like that . . . it was a remarkable thing, indeed.

After two weeks, Pleasure was transferred to a children's rehabilitation facility, and it was here that she hooked up with a homebound schoolteacher and resumed her work on a more formal basis. Three months later, she was back at school, still at the top of her class, where she would remain for the rest of her high school years.

For the longest time following the incident, Pleasure worked to understand what had prompted Phelps to attack her in just this way, and about the best she could figure out is that he wanted to put the same kind of hurt on someone else that had been put on him.

"I never did anything to hurt him," she reasons, "so in the beginning I used to think he thought of us as more than friends. There was never anything romantic between us, but maybe that's not how he saw it. But then, the more I thought about, the more I started to think he took it two or three steps further than that. I think he wanted somebody to be like him, and I was an easy target. He can't walk, ever again, and now here I am scarred forever. He wanted someone to be in the same predicament *he's* in."

Meanwhile, folks started to notice the astonishing ways Pleasure had jumped back into high school. She kept pretty much to herself—to this day, she has a hard time trusting people—but by every other measure, she was a model student with an impeccable grade point average and unfailing initiative and drive.

She was a walking inspiration to anyone who cared to notice, and many did. In fact, when she returned to school late in 1997, three and a half months after the incident, school, law enforcement and child-welfare officials arranged for Pleasure to move to a safer neighborhood in Indiana where she could attend one of the region's top high schools, but she wanted to stay on at Englewood.

"What difference would it have made if I'd switched schools?" she says now. "Nobody can cheat death. If something was meant to happen to me, it would happen to me. I didn't want to live in fear, or feel like I was hiding out."

And for all the talk about how Englewood Technical was the bottom of the bottom, Pleasure was proud to help the school's reputation in her own small way.

"All along, Englewood was known as the worst school you could go to," she says, "the last place you'd want to send your kids, but there was a group of us there starting to turn that all around. Our standardized test scores were off the chart, at least as far as Englewood had ever been concerned. So once I saw I was flourishing there, and that people around me were flourishing, I saw no reason to leave. That was my foundation. People knew me."

Pleasure's got an infectious smile that runs about a mile wide, and you'd never know the terrors she lives with just to look at her. In fact, in her long-sleeved shirts and pants outfits, or her long dresses, many folks don't have any idea what she's been through.

"The only parts of my body that are not scarred are my face and my arms," she explains, "so I'm blessed with that. Even in summer, in 90-degree weather, I'll have on a pair of pants. I don't go to the beach or go swimming, and that's about the only pain that's still with me. There's no physical pain, not anymore. My skin is still not fully stretched out, but I can stand up straight now. I can walk up stairs, and bend over to tie my shoes. I jog a little bit every day to stay in shape. There's nothing that's unbearable. But what I can't bear is seeing another girl my age, my size, with the prettiest pair of shorts, or a really nice bathing suit. Just knowing I will never be that girl again. It pains me to see young girls, girls who have everything going on for them, disrespecting their bodies, disrespecting themselves. It's like they're here for no reason. I cherish that I'm here, and I hope to do something with my life. And I cherish my body. My body is my temple."

When she graduated from Englewood Technical, still at the top of her class, Pleasure got a congratulatory letter from an unexpected supporter. President Bill Clinton wrote to tell her she was "a powerful example of her age," and to tell her he wanted to meet her on his next trip to Chicago to congratulate her personally. And he did. On July 30, 2000, on the tarmac at O'Hare Airport, accompanied by her principal, Samuel Williams, Jr., Pleasure greeted the President just outside Air Force One.

"He told me he was proud of me, and to stay on track," she remembers, and then he posed for pictures taken with Pleasure's disposable camera.

"I can't tell you what it's meant to have so many supportive people behind me," she offers. "Even the President of the United States. It gives me so much pride and joy, but it also keeps me on my toes and focused. Because what it means, really, is now there are also so many people to disappoint, and I'm not about to do that."

Right now, with her first year of core classes out of the way at the University of Chicago, Pleasure's looking ahead to a career in law. She intends to major in political science, and hopes someday to preside as a justice of the United States Supreme Court. Pretty lofty ambitions, were they to come from anyone else, but I get the sense that Pleasure Heard is not the type of young woman to set her mind on a thing unless she means to accomplish it.

"It's like I said all along," she affirms. "God knew I could handle this. That was always my perspective. Everyone was always coming up to me, looking at the bad side, but I refused to look at the bad side. What's done was done, and I had to go on from there. I had to live with things from there."

❀ ❀ ❀

The University of Chicago

"One thing no one can ever take away from me is my education."

Irving Roth stands proudly in front of the Holocaust Resource Center.

CHAPTER EIGHT

Survivor

One of the greatest gifts we can give our children is the gift of history, and this is especially true when an understanding of that history can lend our children a compassionate perspective. This is why I believe it's so incredibly important for young African-American children to discover and celebrate their family histories, dating back a generation or two to the civil rights movement, and all the way back to the time of the Civil War, so that they might fully appreciate what slavery must have meant to their ancestors, and what racism and discrimination must have meant to their parents and grandparents.

Irving Roth, director of the Holocaust Resource Center at Temple Judea in Manhasset, New York, brings this same kind of thinking to his position as one of the leading Holocaust educators in the New York area, maintaining that if we don't talk about the hatred and prejudice that led to the systematic murder of more than six million European Jews during World War II, we might find ourselves heading down a similar road in the not-too-distant future. It's a message that rings true for thousands of young people each year, because Irv delivers it with the kind of firsthand, unvarnished authority that only a Holocaust survivor can bring to the task.

Irv comes to this effort because he is powerless against it. Because it is the right thing to do. The *only* thing to do. For the past 30 or so years, he's made himself available to school and library groups, senior citizens, teachers, civic leaders, friends, neighbors . . . anyone who has cared to listen to his story and his message. He does this as a kind of calling, and now that he's retired from his engineering job at Unisys, it's a *full-time* calling—and a lifetime in the making.

See, back in 1944, when the Allies were winning the war, 14-year-old Irving Roth was removed with most of his family from their temporary home in Hungary, where they had fled from Czechoslovakia some years earlier to escape persecution. They were taken by cattle car with the rest of the Jews in their village to Auschwitz, where they were herded off the train and marched along the railroad platform. At a checkpoint, young Irving, his brother, and two cousins were sent to the left; his grandparents, his aunt and his younger cousins were sent to the right. That night, 3,500 Jews on the "wrong" side of the line—men, women, and children—were forced to undress, corralled into a sealed room, and gassed to death. Their bodies were moved to a crematorium within the same building, and when Irv woke up the next morning, his grandparents, his aunt, and his young cousins had been reduced to smoke and ashes.

"I survived," Irv reflects. "I was lucky. I was given a pair of striped pants and a striped jacket, and was marched off the next morning. Always in line, always in formation. Being counted over and over again for days. Finally, after three days, the conversion of Irving Roth, the person, was complete. I went from being a human being, with a name, to a number. I became a number, and to make sure I remembered that number, they put it on my arm. Branded me. Like an animal."

The branding, and the hateful, uncivilized treatment, were all part of an elaborate process of dehumanization, Irv contends, and in his talks on the subject, he walks his listeners through that process so that they can understand how otherwise respectable, responsible, God-fearing individuals could carry out such unspeakable crimes against humanity.

"Why does it matter," he asks, "to talk about the Holocaust? Why do I do what I do? Because the Holocaust was the ultimate evil. There was no fundamental basis for it. No economic gain, no political gain, no military gain. It was simply prejudice carried to the ultimate, and I want to chronicle the intersection of the lies and the myths and the propaganda, so that altogether you can see the path from prejudice to genocide. That's why it's so important. To show how you can take a little prejudice and, step-by-step, ordinary human beings become capable of extraordinary crimes and still consider themselves to be law-abiding citizens. The objective is to see the signposts along the way."

And so, Irv has made it his life's work—or, at least, his late-in-life's work—to highlight those signposts, and to root them in some of the contemporary ills of our society.

At the close of every presentation he makes on the subject, Irv asks his audience for two things. It doesn't matter if it's a one-on-one meeting with a walk-in visitor to the resource center, or a school visit to several hundred students, the request is the same.

"I tell the students, the next time they're confronted with an incident of prejudice to stand up and do something about it," he says. "It doesn't matter how small or trivial that incident might be. If they're sitting in the cafeteria and someone says, 'Don't let so-and-so sit here, he's too fat,' they must put a stop to it. Why? You've now created a new category of people, called *fat*, and you've decided you don't like it. So, first you don't let them sit at your table, and then you create a separate place in the cafeteria for them to sit, and then you don't let them play sports, and you do a whole bunch of things. They stop being part of your society. You ostracize them. You announce that fat people can't conduct business with people who are not fat. Fat doctors can't operate on people. Step-by-step, to the extreme point where you can finally say, 'They're not perfect human beings, let's kill them.' It sounds extreme, I know, and irrational, but a little prejudice, a little propaganda, and that's how it happens. It's happened before, so you must do something about it before it happens again. Stand up. Be counted. Sure, it's easy to walk away, but for heaven's sake, don't. If you see injustice, do something about it. It doesn't matter who's being picked on, what group is being picked on. When I was a boy, it was the Jews. Tomorrow, it could be somebody else, someone with blond hair and blue eyes. The next day, someone who is black. None of us are safe until every one of us is safe."

The second thing Irving Roth asks of his listeners is to share his story with someone else. Now, and in the future. Find a friend, or family member—or, better yet, a group of friends or family members—and tell them. Write it down so you don't forget. And when his listeners have children of their own, and those children are old enough to understand, Irv charges them to make sure *they* understand, and when those children have children, make sure they understand as well.

"In 30 years, we won't be around anymore to tell our stories," Irv notes of his fellow survivors, "which is why it's so terribly important that these stories don't die with us."

It's hard not to get emotional when you listen to Irving Roth speak of his experience during the war, or the life-and-death struggles of his family, but that's precisely why his message is so powerful. He lived his message, which makes it impossible to look away, and as he talks to his young students in particular, his experiences resonate beyond the words in the textbooks, beyond the fading images in photographs, beyond the newspaper headlines. His words make the unreal all too real. He puts a human face to an inhuman tragedy.

Once, on a trip to Auschwitz with an American youth group, Irv joined with Holocaust educators, historians, and survivors on a tour of the death camps. "By the time they got to Auschwitz," he recalls, "the kids were absorbed with death, corpses, and skeletons. And as we walked through the museum there, we started looking at the posters and signs that remained on the walls. On one of the posters was my name. We were in the Hungarian block of the building, and it was a list of all the people who had survived the first selection in Auschwitz. And there was my name! The students couldn't believe it. At this point, their total minds were lost in thoughts of death, and it occurred to me that when they got home, that would be the image they carried with them, and I didn't think that was the right image. Or, not the sufficient image. I wanted them to know that these were human beings who were murdered. Not just numbers. Not just statistics. So I pointed out my name to them and started telling them a story. I told them about my grandfather, whose name wasn't on that list. He was murdered in Auschwitz, and I told them his story so they would see him not just as a corpse, but as a human being."

In this moving exchange, Irv found the kernel of an idea, and when he returned home, he grew that notion into one of the most successful initiatives in contemporary Holocaust education: the Holocaust Resource Center's Adopt-a-Survivor program. The goal of the project is disarmingly simple—for students to connect, one-on-one, with a survivor in their area, and to spend several hours on a shared journey through that survivor's life.

"The idea," Irv explains, "is to take in that person's total environment, from when he was a baby, to a small child, and so on. To understand the workings of the survivor's home village, his extended family, his place in society. To know his friends and his family. Ideally, the interview sessions are conducted in the survivors' homes, but they can be done in schools, or at our resource center, and the students become biographers. But more than that, they come to know the total person. They become friends. When a friend tells you a story, you don't forget it. You read something in a book or listen to a lecture, and maybe some of it doesn't stay with you. But one-on-one, friend-to-friend, you remember."

Participating students come to understand the total Holocaust experience from the perspective of their adopted survivor. The one life is placed in historical context, and student-biographers are expected to keep a journal of these sessions, reflecting both their own thoughts and the thoughts of their survivor. But here again, the mandate is to share the survivor's story with the next generation, for students to tell their children or nieces and nephews and later their grandchildren, about that survivor. Specifically, in the year 2045, exactly 100 years after the concentration camps stopped belching out smoke, participants are asked to get up in front of a group—school, church, synagogue, community or family gathering, and share the story once more.

"Will they do it?" Irv wonders. "I expect they will. I don't know for certain, but I expect they will. I *hope* they will."

Since the program was launched several years ago, hundreds of survivors have come forward to participate, and each has reportedly found the process rewarding and worthwhile. For the students, too, it's been a life-changing experience. "They don't see things the same way after they hear someone's story," Irv says. "I'll tell you that."

A great many survivors have spent the past 60 or so years closing off that part of their lives, unable to talk about their experiences with their own families, but even these good people have embraced the opportunity to finally go through these motions, in just this way. Irv's even put himself up for "adoption" on many occasions, most recently with an assist from our technological age. What happened was that he hooked up with a student in Manson, Washington, a fairly remote part of the state that happened to have a state-of-the-art video conferencing center to enable students to reach out to outside educators and students. Irv found a video conference facility on the C.W. Post campus of Long Island University, and submitted to several hours-long sessions with the student and the rest of her class. For months prior to the first session, the

A

D
O
Z
E
N

W
A
Y
S

T
O

S
U
N
D
A
Y

140

Manson students read books on the Holocaust, conducted various independent research projects, and created artwork and poetry as an emotional outlet. They also became familiar with Roth's personal history so that they could use the video-conferencing time to full advantage.

"It really was a remarkable thing," Irv reflects, "to talk to this wonderful group of students all the way across the country as if we were in the same room together. I was on a monitor in their classroom, they were on a monitor in the room I was in, and it was as if we were speaking across a table."

In a series of e-mails prior to his "appearance," Irv wrote to his sponsoring student, Kirsten Schwader, about how he and his brother schemed to save the life of their cousin after the three of them had been separated from the rest of their family. Each day, as more and more people from their group were sent off to the gas chamber, the boys realized that the Jews who survived tended to be bigger and stronger than the ones who did not; the thin and the frail were typically the ones singled out for execution. Irv's cousin happened to be short for his age, and the boys constantly worried that he would be among the next group sent to their deaths, so the cousins began carrying bricks with them, whenever they were moved in lines, from one end of the camp to another. When they were made to stand in formation, or stand at attention for inspection, the boys made sure to be in the middle of the pack so that they might stack the bricks to make a step, adding a couple of inches to their cousin's height, and hopefully allowing him to live to see another day.

It was the sort of compelling detail the students from Washington won't soon forget, like something out of a movie, but what made the image of these three young boys scrambling to survive so indelible was the fact that it was delivered by someone who had lived it. That's the power of this "Adopt-a-Survivor" concept, because each survivor has the same kind of compelling details in plenty. After all, they *survived*, and in order to have done so, they had to have been brave and resourceful and stoic and hopeful and resilient and strong. And they had to have a will to live.

"I never wanted to die," Irv reflects. "I always wanted to live. Even after I was separated from my brother and my cousins. Even after my grandparents were murdered. I was happy to be alive. I thought maybe someday life would be better. Like it was when I was a boy. It sounds strange to say it now, but I wanted to live to be able to tell people what was happening. I didn't think anybody would believe it, what I was seeing, so that was a part of it, too."

The other flagship effort at the Holocaust Resource Center has been The Nita Lee Memorial Art Project, named for one of the center's founders and launched on Irv's theory that students can better understand a pivotal event in world history if they have a chance to express their thoughts on that event in artistic ways—through painting, sculpture, and poetry. It's an unconventional approach that has so far won raves from participating high schools throughout the New York area. Each year, the center invites art students from eight to ten high schools for a 20-hour course of study and workshop activities. There's always a theme. This year, it was an exploration of the life and legacy of Janusz Korczak, the Polish-born doctor, educator, humanist, and writer who devoted his life, and his death, to the neglected orphans of the Warsaw ghetto.

As a prominent member of Warsaw society during the war years, Korczak was offered the chance to escape, but he chose instead to accompany 200 or so Jewish children by train from the orphanage he ran to the death camps at Treblinka, offering strength and comfort along the way, all the while knowing that he would die alongside these children. Korczak's story, which I had never heard until Irv told it to me, is a truly moving, inspirational tale of one man's utter devotion to a cause that was bigger than he was. In the hands of Irv's student-artists, it was brought beautifully back to life. And now, in the main hall of the resource center, Irv proudly displays the 60 works of art—watercolors, ceramic and wire sculptures, line drawings, and poems—all reflecting one aspect of Korczak's ennobling life and death.

"To create art," Irv maintains, "you have to internalize your subject. You must have the objective of understanding. To create art about the Holocaust, kids must be intimately involved with the Holocaust. To create, they must feel. Not just know, but actually *feel* what it was like to live at that time, in those conditions. To interpret and internalize, you need the total person. That's the concept Behind Adopt-a-Survivor, and that's what we did here. Our students adopted Janusz Korczak and his orphans until they became a part of them."

The main work of the center, however, focuses on the tours and presentations offered daily to school and civic groups. Last year, by Irv's count, more than 10,000 people walked through the doors of the center and attended a lecture or symposium. The centerpiece of each group visit, naturally, is the firsthand account of a Holocaust survivor, and Irv guesses he offers three or four such talks himself in any given week.

"I don't want to tell you the exact amount," he jokes, "because then my wife will know." His wife of 50 years, Adeline, has been an ardent supporter of Irv's dedication to Holocaust education, even providing the narration for some of the documentaries he's produced, but she worries that all of this living in the past can't be good for her husband. She's afraid that it takes something out of him. All of their other "retired" friends are out on the golf course, or visiting their grandchildren, or wintering in Florida, but Irv is at this thing full time, all year long. When school's in session, he usually schedules two to three groups each day; evenings, there's often an adult education class on the calendar. Even during summer months, there's no letup; this past summer, for example, the Center hosted a touring Anne Frank exhibit in its museum space, and visitor levels soared.

From time to time, Irv's calling even takes him outside the Resource Center and into the community. Like the time several years ago when a couple of punks broke into one of the local schools and painted swastikas on the wall. A rabbi, a priest, and a social worker were brought in to speak to these kids.

"No one could get through to them," Irv explains. "They were totally defiant. So finally the person in charge of straightening these kids out asked me to come in and talk to them. They looked at me in a way that said, 'I don't want to be here. I'd rather go to jail than listen to you, old man.' It was a very tense, very difficult situation, and it was the only time in my life I used shock treatment. I said to the one who seemed to be the leader, 'Do you have a brother?' He said, 'Yeah, what's it to you?' I said, 'Is he blond, and does he have blue eyes?' He said, 'Yeah, what's it to you?' I said, 'Well, tomorrow, we're going to hang him.' All of a sudden, this kid's demeanor changed. 'You can't do that!' he shouted back at me. But I said, 'Oh, yes, we can. We only allow one blond, blue-eyed person per family.' Again, the boy shouted out, 'You can't do that!' He became enraged, and I explained to him that this is just what happened to my brother. They killed him for what he was. A Jew. And as I spoke, there was this remarkable transformation. This kid realized, for the first time in his life, I think, that this swastika symbol was real, that killing Jews was real, and that it applied to him. He and his friends had no idea. It was just a symbol to them. Something they had seen, somewhere, totally unconnected to the Holocaust."

I'll end this passage in the same way Irv closes out his own Holocaust odyssey—on a hopeful note. By April of 1945, Irv had been transferred to another concentration camp, at Buchenwald, where he and his fellow prisoners were made to break rocks all day long. He would look around at the prisoners alongside him and figure out which ones would last the day, or the week. People were dying of hunger or sickness. Or, if they appeared to be too weak, they were being shot. "You could see them disintegrating right before your eyes," he says.

Irv banded together with a group of other kids around the same age, and together they determined that the path to survival was to stay put. There were more than 50,000 prisoners at Buchenwald, and each day, 5,000 to 10,000 were pulled from their ranks and marched off to their deaths. Irv and his friends determined that the thing to do was hide out on the camp grounds and avoid the selection process. And so, they did. Under buildings. In sewers. Wherever they could squeeze their tiny, emaciated bodies. Each day, the hope was that the U.S. Army would come in and save them. And eventually, that's just what happened. On April 10, 1945, Irv was no longer able to hide. The Germans had unleashed guard dogs to sniff them out, and Irv and his friends stood among 10,000 others waiting to be directed to their fate when air sirens sounded. Irv heard the whir of airplanes overhead.

It seemed to him to be some sort of air raid at first, and before he realized what was happening, the guards began to disperse. One guard started shooting at prisoners as he fled, but he eventually ran out of bullets, and when the noise turned to silence, the prisoners wandered back to their barracks. There was no place else to go.

The next day, April 11th, the prisoners weren't awakened at three in the morning, as was usually the case. At nine o'clock, they still hadn't been called from quarters. At eleven, Irv heard rounds being fired in the distance, and a short time later, three or four American soldiers walked into the barracks. They looked around, these hardened GI's, took in the devastating scene, and cried.

But Irv's story didn't end with his liberation. He walked around what was left of Buchenwald until he found someone he had gone to school with back in Czechoslovakia, and together they decided to return to their home village to see if any of their friends or family had survived. Irv knew he had lost his brother, his grandparents, his aunt, and his cousins, but he had no word about his parents. His father had taken ill, in Budapest, prior to the mass removal of Jews from Hungary, with his mother at his side, so Irv had no idea if they were alive or dead. He allowed himself to hope that by some miracle they had escaped—and indeed, they had. He found them living in a house not far from where he grew up, and with them he also found a story that allowed him to think that there was still some goodness in the world.

"There was a night nurse at my father's hospital in Budapest," Irv explains, "and as my father lay in a coma, she would talk to him. Every night she would talk to him. She was a Seventh Day Adventist, and her thinking was, *Who knows? Perhaps he can understand.* So, she talked. And, in fact, one night he awoke from his coma as if nothing had happened. He didn't know that Jews were being pulled from their homes, and that his whole family had been taken away. But my mother knew, and the nurse knew, and they wound up going to this nurse's home, to a one-bedroom apartment she shared with her daughter and granddaughter. Her son-in-law was off fighting for the Nazis, but this woman was proof that not everyone was a Nazi. Not everyone did as they were told. There were some good people, willing to stick their necks out and help, and this nurse was one of them. She hid my parents in her apartment, and it was very dangerous for her to do that. The Nazis used to come by and search for Jews, but she kept them out of sight. In January of 1945, the Russian army liberated Budapest, and my parents were once again free to move about and return to their lives, but it was only possible because of the kindness of this wonderful lady. She only saved two people, but they were two very important people to me. There were nine million people living in Hungary at that time, and only about 200 individuals or families helped or hid Jews. That's not everything, I realize, but it's something."

The lesson, for Irving Roth and the thousands of annual visitors to the Holocaust Resource Center, is that even in the face of blind oppression, abject hatred, and full-scale genocide, an act of simple human kindness can prevail. It might not be *everything*, but it will be *something*—and if enough of us take up this same notion, it will be something else, to be sure.

❀ ❀ ❀

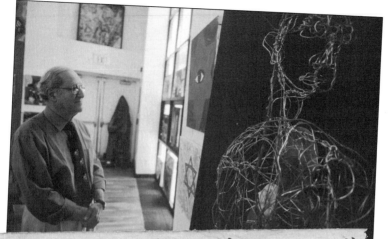

Irving looks forward to keeping the story alive through art and education.

Irving explains the encased art that represents victims of the Holocaust.

Irving in front of the most current exhibit profiling Dr. Janusz Korczak, who is remembered for helping children through the Holocaust tragedy.

Irving shares some of the students' artwork at the Holocaust Resource Center.

Sulieman Beyah reaches out with "Smiling Hands" to help other chronically ill children.

CHAPTER NINE

Smiling Hands

Sometimes big ideas come wrapped in small packages.

Consider the story of Sulieman Beyah, a remarkable young man from Philadelphia who looked on his own chronic illness as an opportunity to help other kids struggling through something similar.

Sule, as his mom calls him, was eight years old when he started experiencing some unusual symptoms. He'd hardly been sick a day in his life, had never missed school, and was about as active as an eight-year-old kid had any right to be. In fact, he'd just come back from a dynamite trip to Hawaii to celebrate his grandmother's 50th birthday, where he'd spent the whole week sightseeing, playing on the beach, bicycling, taking pictures, and basically having the time of his young life. He thought it was about the best vacation he could have ever imagined—going to a place where even the garbage smelled like pineapples.

But when he returned home and resumed his day-to-day routines, Sulieman started to notice that he was always tired. It was a constant, nagging thing. Every step he took, he was dragging. He managed to make it through school okay, but in the afternoons, when he went to a neighbor's house to do his homework while his mother worked, he'd fall asleep on the couch. Despite the fatigue, he stayed on top of his assignments, same as he always did. You see, Sulieman had been skipped ahead a couple years in school, and had tested off-the-charts into whatever gifted or accelerated programs they had at his level, so he took a special pride in getting his work done on time. And it wasn't enough just to get the work done; he had to get it done right. Still, he'd go home and head straight for bed. On weekends, he'd sleep all day. The all-encompassing fatigue was accompanied by rapid weight loss—about 15 pounds in just a couple of weeks, so Sulieman's mother took him to the pediatrician for a thorough checkup.

"At the time, we weren't too worried, my mom and me," Sulieman recalls. "We just thought I was overdoing it and that the tiredness was catching up to me. At first the doctor didn't appear too worried, either. It was just like any other annual physical. He went over my entire chart, asked like a million questions, and took my blood and my urine and was about to send me home. Then one of the nurses came in to tell the doctor they'd found too much protein in my urine. Right away, the doctor became real concerned, and he told us to set up an appointment with a nephrologist to see what was going on with my kidneys, but we couldn't get in to see this guy for the longest time."

It took about a month for that appointment to roll around, even after some string-pulling by the pediatrician, and during that time, Sulieman started experiencing some debilitating back pains. He still wasn't missing any school or falling behind on his work, but these bouts were getting the better of him. One night, the pain was so bad that his mom came in to find Sulieman doubled over in a fetal position, and she collected him in her arms and rushed him to the emergency room, where after another full workup, the emergency room doctors also told them that Sule had to see a nephrologist. They hurried over to Children's Hospital of Philadelphia—CHOP, for short—where they felt that Sule would receive better, more age-appropriate care, and they had their diagnosis soon enough: lupus, an auto-immune disorder that basically leaves the body attacking its own connective tissue. There is no known cure, but the disease can sometimes be controlled with steroids and other strong medications. Lupus patients can go into long periods of remission, but the disease can flare up at any time.

In Sulieman's case, this meant a heavy-duty dose of cytoxin, which is often used in the chemo-like treatment of cancer patients; and solumedrol, a steroid that can sometimes cause dangerous mood swings. It also meant a 24-hour blood pressure monitor; dialysis; and various seizures, setbacks, and uncertainties. And, ultimately, it meant an all-but-complete shutdown of both kidneys.

Almost immediately, Sulieman's mom arranged for family members to get themselves checked to see if they were a suitable match for a kidney donation. Happily, Sulieman's uncle stepped up as a viable donor, and the wheels were put in motion for a transplant, but a variety of complications forced them to scrap those plans and look for another kidney. First, Sulieman took ill just before the scheduled transplant, then his uncle developed a virus just before the rescheduled transplant, and then it was determined that his uncle had high blood pressure and wouldn't be able to donate at all. Sulieman's kidneys were operating at about 20 percent of capacity, and the need for a new one was becoming more and more urgent.

Meanwhile, Sulieman's behavior became unrecognizable. According to his mom, he was someone else underneath all of these mood-altering steroids. And according to Sule himself, he was out of control. "I would destroy things all the time," he remembers. "Just break things into pieces. Sometimes I'd wreck my entire room. My mother kept complaining to the doctors that I was getting too many steroids. She wanted them to wean me down. But they wanted to be real aggressive. It was a constant battle. Once I grabbed one of my doctors by the tie and started yelling at him to change my medications. They had to call security on me. They called Psych and Social Services. Finally, they realized that this particular medication wasn't right for me, in this particular dosage, and they changed it, but it took a long time, and what we realized was that a lot of doctors aren't willing to look at individual patients on a case-by-case basis. They have a course of treatment in mind, and that's it."

Sulieman's moods were more manageable with the change in medication, but he was still reacting to the steroids. He wasn't eating properly, and he had difficulty sleeping. He kept himself busy—swimming, riding horses, tending to his menagerie of pets—hoping that the cytoxin would arrest the deterioration of his kidneys, or at least slow down the process to allow time for another donor to emerge. By every measure, though, Sulieman's kidneys were failing, and it was only a matter of time before the need moved from urgent to dire. Normally, if you go into renal failure, you're placed on the waiting list for a kidney donor and given a life-support pager so you can be reached at all times, but Sule and his mom had all these other options in the works with family and friends, and they thought they'd beat the waiting list, so they'd never gotten hooked up with a pager.

On the afternoon of June 11, 2000, though, Sulieman's name came up as a match, and Sule and his mom were nowhere to be found. They'd taken their dogs for a bath and a swim at a friend's pool, and the hospital staff was frantically calling all of their contact numbers, trying to track them down.

When word finally reached Sule and his mom, he broke down crying. All along, he'd been thinking he'd have some time to prepare himself for the transplant, to get used to the idea, but here it was, now or never. "It kinda caught me by surprise," he says now. "I wasn't ready. It was late in the afternoon. I hadn't eaten anything all day. We were getting set to go out to Jersey to eat some crabs, and we were kinda looking forward to that, and then, with this one call, everything changed. It snuck up on me, basically. It wasn't what I was expecting."

By the time that Sulieman reached the hospital, the waiting room was filled with friends and family, but they would have to wait awhile longer for good news. After all of that waiting, and trying to locate the patient, the surgery had to be postponed until the following morning, which meant that Sule's mom still had time to run out to New Jersey to fetch some crabs for 20 or so folks who were back in Sulieman's hospital room keeping him company, getting used to this latest turn of events.

The transplant went off without a hitch, and a year and a half after the surgery, Sule is moving around at just-about full speed. He's active in non-contact sports, rides the city bus home from school each afternoon, looks after his various pets and projects, and by virtually all outward measures, has resumed the life of a typical 13-year-old kid.

Now, here's where Sulieman's story takes a more global turn. This brave young man was spending so much time in Children's Hospital—

for a two-year stretch, his mom calculated, (he spent more time in than out)—that he started to think how fortunate he was to have his mother and grandmother at his side, and to have the resources resulting from their inquiries and constant care. (His parents are divorced, and his father was pretty much out of the picture before Sulieman took ill in the first place.) Without really thinking about it, Sulieman found himself reaching out to other CHOP patients, kids whose parents couldn't always come around, kids who didn't have the money for a toy or a balloon to brighten their room, kids who didn't have anyone to advocate for them with the doctors and nurses.

Sulieman hadn't always been such a giving child, or even such a sensitive one. He'll be the first to tell you that before he got sick, it wasn't unusual to see him at the bullying end of a schoolyard taunt, or at the trouble-making end of one incident or another. He was usually respectful of his elders, but he wasn't always respectful of kids his own age. A lot of times, he was one of the first to tease or taunt. And now, from this new perspective, his impulse was to help other kids negotiate these rough patches— to educate healthy kids on what it's like to live with a chronic illness, or to be caught in the wheelhouse of long-term care. To help erase the teasing and the taunting that comes from a childhood illness or disability. To make a difference for other sick kids in the same way his mom and grandmother had been able to make a difference for him.

Like I said, Sulieman wasn't really thinking these efforts through; they just seemed like the right thing to do each time out. He'd get an idea and see it through. He'd pick up a little something in the gift shop for a new child on the unit, or stop by to spend time with a boy whose family couldn't visit. He'd go around from one room to another, looking for someone who might want him to read to them, or someone who just wanted company while they were watching television. He'd wheel around books from the library for anyone who might want one. Sometimes his mom helped with a special project, but for the most part, he made these efforts on his own. His good work in this regard did not go unnoticed by the CHOP nurses, and soon enough, Sulieman was asked to serve on the hospital's Youth Advisory Council.

In the beginning, he was one of only a half-dozen young people to sit on the council, but Sule and his cohorts have successfully lobbied to have an entire wing of the hospital overhauled and redesigned from a kid-friendly perspective. They've arranged it so that in-patients can order lunch from the on-site McDonald's, or pizza from the on-site Pizza Hut. "And it comes in the box," Sulieman offers proudly, "not on a plate. On a plate, on a tray, it gets all soggy, but when it comes in a box, it's like the real thing."

Just as important, the Youth Advisory Council, which now numbers about 20, conducts a hospital-wide Teen Night every two or three months, complete with games, food, and entertainment, and

Sulieman was asked to make a presentation to hospital administrators on successful methods for young patients to approach their doctors. The presentation was so well received that he's been asked to go back before the full board to deliver his message again. In his presentation, he made particular note of how important it is for doctors to listen to kids in their care, and he pointed to his own difficulties in coping with his steroid dose, and his related frustrations in getting his doctors to respond.

"I was doing all of these things on a small scale," Sulieman notes, "just as they came up, but as I got better myself, and stronger, I started to think about how I could help on a larger scale. There are so many kids in the hospital without their families around for support—not just at Children's Hospital, but all over Philadelphia. All over the country. They can't get the medication they need. Or maybe they come from a single-parent family, and there's no one at home to shop for groceries or look after their siblings. Or maybe there's a language problem, and there's no one to explain a diagnosis or a treatment protocol. Even without a language barrier, there can be some intimidation in dealing with doctors, in not having an advocate who knows what's really going on."

It was at this point that Sulieman reached out to me to help bring his Smiling Hands organization into wider focus. (Incidentally, he first thought to christen his nonprofit effort Helping Hands, but when he found that the name was already being held by another agency, he settled

161

on this more interesting handle.) In his letter to me, Sulieman told me about a friend of his who had recently died after a difficult bout with cancer. What struck this young man, and what struck me on the rebound, was that she had died without a loving network of family and support, or the resources she might have needed to make her last days more comfortable. It was not only that she had suffered, but that she had suffered alone. There wasn't a thought for Sulieman's own ordeal, but for this little girl.

"She had a very sad life," he wrote, and he went on to fill me in on an idea he had to pool various volunteer resources and donations to promote the importance of organ donation and hands-on support for children with chronic illnesses. He had a whole bunch of ideas—most of them good ones—and he laid them all out for me like the no-nonsense kid he is.

His mother, too, sent along an accompanying note, in which she told me of some of Sulieman's extraordinary accomplishments, and his firsthand compassion. "I would like for Sulieman to be able to share his story," she wrote, "so that others may realize that the end is when you stop or say, 'I can't.'"

For the longest time, our producers tried to incorporate Sulieman's vision of caring and support into a show on young people making a difference in the world around them, but we never seemed to be able to put together the right mix of kids, on the right schedule, so when this book project rolled around, it seemed like the perfect time to shine a light on this young man, and on his example.

Here are Sulieman's words, from his own book on his ordeal, *Thru My Eyes,* which he hopes to publish and distribute to raise funds for Smiling Hands:

> I remember this very nasty medicine that I would have to drink after each treatment. I asked the doctor if he had ever tasted it. It was horrible. Even the smell made me sick. It smelled like poop and vomit together. The doctor explained that the medicine kept me from bleeding internally, but if I could promise him that I would drink enough water to flush out my system, I wouldn't have to drink it. I made the promise, and I kept it, because anything was better than having to drink that awful medicine.

In a way, the "awful medicine" of Sulieman's experience is a kind of tonic for sick kids all over Philadelphia—and if Sule has his way, all over the country. He's hung on to share his story and his perspective—and he's holding out his "smiling" hands to guide other children with chronic illnesses down his path of positive thinking and boundless good cheer.

Good for him.

And good for the rest of us, too.

❋ ❋ ❋

Sulieman with his mom,
Lucretia Beyah.

Sulieman—now recovered and making a difference.

83-year-old certified aerobics instructor Arnold C. Bull.

CHAPTER TEN

Longevity in Action

*H*ere's a story to lift your spirits—and get your heart pumping.

Meet Arnold Bull, World War II veteran, retired swimming pool products salesman, father of seven, and all-around good guy, who at 69 years of age found himself overweight, bored, and about as physically unfit as a man had any right to be this side of a hospital or an old-age home. (*This side* meaning the *out*side.)

Now, at 83, Arnold's the oldest certified aerobics instructor in the United States, 50 pounds lighter than he was at his worst, 50 years younger in his outlook, and a poster boy for the get-up-and-go that has gotten-up-and-left too many of our older friends, neighbors, and family members. And he offers up the kind of inspiration that gets results—for himself, and for the thousands of seniors who've taken one of his classes, listened to one of his lectures, or read about him in one of their local newspapers.

Talk about building a body of work. In nearly 15 years as an aerobics instructor, Arnold's helped to turn around the lives of countless seniors, one body at a time. In the bargain, he's also changed the shape of his own life, and he and his students are all the richer for it.

"Sixty-five percent of all chronic illnesses that kill people prematurely are preventable," Arnold lets me know, with the infectious good cheer and high-voltage energy that have become his calling cards. "And how are they preventable? With good nutrition, proper exercise, and staying away from the idea of being a couch potato. That's what kills us quicker than anything. Sitting still. Not doing anything. I took early retirement at 62, and before I knew it, almost everyone I knew— all my relatives who were my peers, all of my friends, most of my army buddies, and with one or two exceptions, all of my business associates— were dead. I thought to myself, *Arnold, you've got to do something.*"

Of course, human nature being what it is, Arnold didn't do much with this realization beyond setting it aside. The real push wouldn't come for a few years into his retirement, when Arnold's beautiful wife, Alice, was diagnosed with colon cancer, and even though she beat it with successful surgery and managed to avoid chemotherapy, Arnold saw his wife's illness as the wake-up call he needed to jump-start the rest of their lives together. He sat with his wife's doctors and started asking questions. He wondered if the cancer could return, if there were any precautions Alice could take to improve her chances, if there were aspects of his own diet and lifestyle he should consider changing to avoid the same fate, and he wound up with so many different opinions that he guessed that the thing to do was hit the books and figure things out for himself.

"I read every book I could find, every journal article, every newsletter," he says of his crash-course in self-directed study. "I went to every lecture. Gee whiz, sometimes I had to sneak in wearing a stethoscope around my neck just to look the part. I focused mainly on preventive medicine, and after a while, I started studying nutrition. I read everything I could find on it. Remember, I was retired, so I had a lot of time on my hands. It took just a few days of staying home and watching soap operas for me to realize that this wasn't for me, so this was just the thing."

The more Arnold learned about exercise and nutrition, the more he put what he was learning into practice. He joined the local YMCA and started to lose weight. He stopped smoking and cut down on his drinking. He took up power walking. He did water aerobics. He encouraged Alice to do the same, and she gladly obliged; the Bulls went from a fairly sedentary existence to an all-out active lifestyle. Arnold found it ironic that, for a guy who spent his career in and around the swimming pool industry, it took his retirement to use a pool for good health instead of just for good times. He began to feel better than he'd felt since his days in the service, and started to greet each day like there was something in it for him. As a businessman, Arnold describes himself as a real "rounder": "I could have gone into any major airport in any major city in the country, walked into the bar, and the bartender would have known exactly what I would have ordered, just by seeing me coming. I wasn't a falling-down alcoholic, just a guy out there doing what everyone else was doing. And those fabulous expense-account meals? You know what that's like. So let's just say I wasn't in the best of shape."

No, he wasn't, but he was determined to change. And Alice, God bless her, was with Arnold every step of the way. They exercised together, watched what they ate together, and relocated together to a retirement community in North Carolina, where they felt they could enjoy some milder weather than what was usually available to them on the New Jersey shore. One afternoon, while Arnold was working out in the swimming pool at his new health club, the manager approached him and asked Arnold if he'd get some of the older folks together to form a class.

Arnold was new to the community, and so he saw this as a great way to reach out and meet some new people. He marshaled his easy enthusiasm and started talking up the benefits of water aerobics. Before he knew it, there was a class. People seemed excited to work out with other people their own age. It was a little intimidating working out alongside all those young, hard bodies they had down at the health club. But Arnold's group was looking to move at an easy pace, and they didn't care if they turned heads so much as they were looking to turn their lives around. Soon enough, Arnold emerged as the de facto leader of the group, and he signed on for an intensive course of study offered by the University of North Carolina to receive his certification as an aerobics instructor.

"They were astounded that a man would enroll in a program like this," Arnold recalls. "There were maybe 120 of us in the course, and I was the only male in the bunch. Come to think of it, I was the only one over 30!"

I'd never really thought about it before, until I met Arnold, but aerobics instructors *do* tend to be young and female. But that didn't stop Arnold Bull from graduating in the top 25 percent of his class, and embarking on a second career that didn't promise a whole lot of money, but offered a path to the kind of healthy, purposeful living that had eluded him as a younger man. Certification in hand, he started teaching for the city of Charlotte, and then at various apartment complexes, and eventually at the YMCA. It got to where he was leading 16 classes a week, which is a whole lot of classes when you realize that aerobics instructors are out in front, putting themselves through the same motions as their students. Conventional medical wisdom holds that, for seniors, three sessions a week is about what you need to stay fit. Actually, this is the minimum recommended course for all adults, regardless of age, but it seems harder to accomplish the longer we put it off.

So there was Arnold, in his mid-70s, doing more than five times the recommended exercise for a man his age, and a little bit more besides, because in addition to his classes, he also lifted weights at home. "I'm a firm believer in weight training," he insists. "The only problem, for an older person, is that free weights are not a good idea. Older folks are too unstable; it's too easy for them to fall over while they're doing it, so I always recommend a cross-training machine. Universal, Nautilus—anything to get rid of that danger."

A couple months into his new routines, and Arnold was supremely fit—but more than that, so was his wife. And so were his charges. His classes were filled to waiting-list proportions (200 strong, at their longest), and his students were reinvigorated by his approach. One of the things you realize as you get older is that it's not so easy to reinvent the wheel each time out, and once Arnold accepted that his workout routines would pretty much stay the same from one class to the next, he looked for ways to vary his classes in order to keep things interesting.

"I thought, *Boy, this is gonna get boring,*" he explains, "so I started making my own tapes. I must have 1,500 old vinyl records, of every style of music imaginable, and I put together all kinds of tapes. Marching band, rock 'n' roll, honky-tonk, ragtime, big band. If I can get 80 beats a minute out of it, that's all I need. We'll hear the music come on, and I'll sing the lyrics, or we'll all start singing, and reminiscing. 'Gosh, when's the last time I heard that?' Sometimes the music is just the push we need. If it's Christmastime, I'll throw in a little something special for the occasion. Fourth of July, I'll play some John Philip Sousa. It keeps us all on our toes."

Arnold's combination of invigorating, nostalgic music, suitable for sing-a-longs; and his cheerful approach to fitness and wellness, have made his classes wildly popular. He's even expanded his efforts to include a series of motivational talks he presents to groups all over the East Coast, on topics ranging from osteoporosis to cooking.

"Stop thinking about getting old," Arnold preaches. "You know you're old, but stop thinking about it. It's a foregone conclusion for a lot of people—you reach a certain age, now it's time to start dying. My motto is, life is a lot like driving. You slow down before you come to a stop. Slow down if you have to, but keep driving. You can keep going and going and going. Age is not a disease. It's just another stage of life, and just like every other stage of life, if you don't use it, you'll lose it. It doesn't matter if it's your brain or your body. Keep active. It's silly to say, 'Oh, that doesn't interest me anymore.' Why not? It becomes a self-fulfilling prophecy. I see these older women wearing these librarian shoes, and I tell them to get out and see what other women their age or older are wearing. Their mothers never wore sneakers, but they're wearing sneakers today. They're active, and out there, and doing things."

Another of Arnold's mottos, "Longevity in Action," is imprinted on the T-shirts he wears to his classes, and it stands as a reminder that you need to keep moving if you want to keep living. "Anybody can live long," he says, "but to live long and stay healthy, to stay out of a wheelchair, to not need a walker or one of those oxygen gadgets up your nose—well, then you've got to be active."

Arnold's extra efforts have not gone unnoticed. He's become something of a local legend. He and Alice eventually returned to New Jersey to be closer to their family (7 children, 15 grandchildren, and 6 great-grandchildren), and he's now teaching five days a week, and lecturing two or three times each week.

However, these days his legend extends beyond the New Jersey shore. In 1999, he was cited by the national Blue Cross and Blue Shield Association as one of six "ageless American heroes," and he was honored at a special ceremony in Chicago by former President George Bush and former First Lady Barbara Bush. Alice and Arnold were even given their own "day" and held up as role models for seniors in Monmouth County, New Jersey. That's where Alice serves as a peer instructor in the Healthy Bones program, sponsored by the New Jersey Department of Health and Senior Services; and Arnold serves as the Health and Fitness Director of the Senior Citizens Activities Network (SCAN). Also, the Bulls were the only couple recognized by Nabisco in the company's annual "Fittest Over Fifty" national search, and for the awards ceremony in New York City, Arnold bused in 50 of his students for photo-opportunity workout sessions in Central Park.

Lately, Arnold's pride and joy has been the all-male aerobics class he leads at SCAN, co-sponsored by the local YMCA. The "Gung-Ho Guys Aerobics Team" grew out of a concern Arnold was having over the fact that senior men were not actively participating in exercise classes—his, or anyone else's. He did a little research on the subject and concluded that older men tended to be self-conscious in classes led by "teeny-bopper" instructors.

"You can't have a grizzled old ex-marine listening to an 18-year-old in spandex and expect to get anywhere," is the way he explains it. The older men were often ashamed of their bodies— "we don't have those six-pack bellies anymore"— and even those who acted on the initial impulse to enroll in an exercise program didn't always have the incentive to see it through. So Arnold set out to change that, and he offered what is believed to be the only all-male, senior citizen aerobics class in the country. He'd been an Army drill instructor, and he thought to fashion these workouts on a military model.

"A lot of these guys were former Army, Navy, Air Force, Marines," he explains. "World War II, Korea, Vietnam vets. They'd reached the age where they were looking to do some of that stuff again in an all-male environment. The first class, we had six guys enrolled. Next time, it doubled. The time after that, we were up to 18. Now we're at 40, and I have to turn people away." The Gung-Ho Guys work out twice a week to Sousa, military marches, and old-time hits, using a lot of the military moves that are familiar to his students. The sessions are macho to the core. At the close of each one, Arnold and company end with their own, locker-room credo: "Every day, in every way, I'm getting leaner and meaner and hornier." Each phrase, Arnold proudly reports, is accompanied by appropriate (or, I should say, *in*appropriate) hand gestures.

"The women are sticking their heads in all the time," Arnold explains. "In the beginning, we got all this flack for keeping things separate, but now they want to come in and watch the men."

As a self-taught, lay nutritionist, Arnold advocates moderation in most diets. He eats a bowl of oatmeal each morning, with a glass of orange juice, a cup of coffee, and half of a grapefruit. For lunch, he favors a salad accompanied by one of the soy protein burgers that are now available at most major supermarkets around the country.

"They're fabulous," Arnold gushes. "When they first came out, they used to be awful, but now they're just wonderful." He'll chase the burger with a non-alcoholic beer or a diet juice drink. For dinner, he'll lean toward poached fish, with a baked potato on the side. "For the most part," he notes, "if you cut down on what you eat, you can eat anything. Most restaurants overfeed their customers. It's like they're trying to kill us. So when Alice and I go out, we order one meal and cut it in half."

Arnold Bull's transformation is an inspiration to anyone who's lived a "retiring" life, and who's looking to recharge their batteries for the years ahead. It's also a case-in-point for couples hoping to stay in good shape as they grow old together, with the kind of positive energy they'll need to sustain the shared bumps along the way.

"We're having the best time of our lives right now," Arnold told a reporter for a local newspaper. "If people are truly in love with each other, this is one of the keys to health and happiness. I don't know if being healthy makes you more lovable, but it does help you love and be loved, and loving and being loved makes you more healthy."

Words to live by, don't you think?

❀ ❀ ❀

Arnold teaches one of his "all-male seniors" classes.

Arnold's stretch for success.

The Gung-Ho Guys
take a breather.

Arnold and his wife, Alice.

Flo and Jim Wheatley with their son, Leonard, at home in Hop Bottom, Pennsylvania.

CHAPTER ELEVEN

A Warm Embrace

This story has a life of its own, and it flows from a single good turn.

Back in 1982, a licensed practical nurse named Flo Wheatley from Hop Bottom, Pennsylvania, was in New York City with her 14-year-old son. The boy had been diagnosed with non-Hodgkin's lymphoma, and he was being treated at Memorial Sloan Kettering in Manhattan, one of the leading cancer-care hospitals in the world.

Flo was not the sort of person then, nor is she the sort of person now, to let a thing like cancer slow her down or dim her sunny outlook. She knew what it was like to be hit by this kind of illness, she understood the diagnosis and the course of treatment, and she looked on her son Leonard's outpatient care at Sloan Kettering as a kind of godsend. Moreover, she was grateful that they could stay with a niece in nearby Queens when they came to town for the treatments.

At the time, poor Leonard wasn't doing too well with his chemotherapy. Hundreds of tumors had spread throughout his body, he was desperately sick, and his prognosis was grim. But Flo put on her brave game face and went about their shared business. "Sometimes," she says, "there are things in this world you just have to take care of."

One Monday afternoon, Leonard was having a particularly tough time after leaving the hospital. It was raining, Flo had their suitcases with them, they were heading out to Queens on the subway, and Leonard pretty much had to drop to the pavement in sickness—right there, in the middle of all kinds of commotion. They were on Lexington Avenue, just a few paces from the subway entrance.

"He couldn't stand," Flo remembers, "so I got him propped up on one of our suitcases and let him retch into a plastic bag. And we stayed there for a while, waiting for Leonard to be able to catch up to himself."

It was during this dark, miserable moment that Flo's life took a fateful turn. Leonard would eventually beat the cancer and go on to partner with his mom in a home-care business, so happily, it wasn't any kind of life-and-death moment. Rather, it was a moment graced by a random act of kindness, tossed at mother and child by a disheveled-looking man who appeared to be homeless.

Flo's "angel," as she's taken to thinking about him, was thin and tall, almost wiry. He wore a pair of ratty blue jeans, old sneakers over his bare feet, and an Army surplus jacket with a mess of honor bars decorating one sleeve. Around his belt, he had a well-stocked key chain, about six inches around, although he didn't seem to be the sort of person in need of so many keys. (Goodness, she'd never seen so many keys on one ring!) He also wore the oddest pair of gold-rimmed glasses Flo Wheatley had ever seen, and what was odd about them was that there was no glass in the frames. They were just the gold rims, and she'll never forget the way the empty frames set off this man's eyes in this weird, melancholy way. There was nothing sinister about this particular man, nothing menacing, but there was definitely something *off*.

"If you spend any time in a place like New York," Flo explains, "as we had to do when Leonard was at Sloan, you can't help but notice how many people are homeless and desperate on the city's streets. There's always someone in a doorway, or on a subway platform, or up against a building trying to get warm. In the beginning, anyway, you notice. You can't help but notice and wonder what you can do to help, but after a while, you realize you can't help everybody. After a while, you start stepping over people just like everyone else."

So this odd-looking man approached Flo, and she was too distracted by Leonard's retching to take him in fully, but he sidled by and said, "You need help, lady." He wasn't asking, he was declaring, and Flo didn't have it in her to agree.

"No," she said. "I'm okay. We're okay. We're fine."

The man wouldn't be put off. He lingered, 10 or 20 feet away, and soon enough, he made another approach. "You need help, lady," he said again.

This time, Flo's good, trusting instincts got the better of her, and she offered a little detail in her response. To a hardened New Yorker, perhaps she offered a little too much, but out in Hop Bottom, folks are a bit more forthcoming. They tell it plain. "That's all right," she said. "We're heading out to Queens. We'll just catch our breath and head for the subway."

At this, the man reached for Flo's suitcase (Leonard was sitting on his), picked it up, indicated for the two of them to follow, and headed down the subway stairs with a bag packed with all of Flo's money for her stay in New York, and all of her clothes. There was nothing for Flo to do but grab Leonard by the hand and head down the stairs after her suitcase. She didn't for a moment think that the man was looking to make off with her things, but she followed as if she was giving chase. It was approaching rush hour, and the station was crowded. For a beat or two, she worried that she might lose him. The man ducked underneath the subway turnstile while Flo took the time to pay for herself and Leonard, and when they reached the platform, the man was waiting. It was too loud to talk, and too crowded to get near, but as Flo moved to thank him, she could see he wasn't finished. He got on the train with them, and when they switched trains at Queens Plaza, the man switched trains, too.

He held her suitcase the entire way. By the time they reached their stop, the rush-hour crowds had thinned, and Flo was able to make herself heard above the din of the subway tunnel. She pressed some money into the man's hands, thanked him for helping her with her suitcase, and walked up the stairs with Leonard to the street.

Naturally, the man followed them. Leonard was still quite sick, and Flo couldn't see waiting for the bus to take them to her niece's apartment, so she hailed a taxi. Or, she tried to, anyway. The first cabbie wouldn't stop. Flo guessed the driver could see the trouble Leonard was in, and wasn't interested in having to clean the back seat of his car after the fare. Her homeless angel must have seen it the same way, because he stepped into the street, directly in front of the next cab he saw, grabbed the door handle, and wouldn't let go as the driver tried to pull away. He ran alongside the car until the driver had to stop, and then he swung the door open, threw Flo's suitcase into the back seat, and motioned for her and Leonard to climb in. "Come on, lady," he said, and when Flo and Leonard were situated in the back seat, he leaned in the window and said, "Don't abandon me."

And that was that. The whole, strangely caring, only-in-New York exchange. Flo held Leonard's hand as they drove away, and she knew she would never forget the man's face, the glassless rims that framed his eyes, and his haunting words as they parted: *Don't abandon me*. She thought to herself, *No, I won't abandon you, but how can I help you? Where will I find you? What do you need?* They got home safely, and Leonard gathered his strength for the next round of chemo. Through it all, Flo saw the hardened face of this benevolent stranger.

Don't abandon me.

Two years later, Flo and Leonard were still going to the city on a fairly regular basis. Sometimes Flo's husband, Jim, made the trip, but more often than not, it was Flo. Leonard's cancer was thankfully in remission, but there were all kinds of follow-up treatments and such, and on one pass through town, driving back out to Queens over the 59th Street Bridge, Flo put two and two together in a way that would change her life forever. She saw another homeless man up against a bridge abutment. She'd seen this same man many times before—this was his spot—but on this day, he happened to be wrapped in a pink crocheted blanket. It was the oddest thing—to see this desperate man cloaked in a pink blanket, and as Flo inched past in traffic, she thought to herself, *Someone must have made that for him.* She heard again the words of her homeless angel—*don't abandon me!*—and it was as if a light went on over her head. *Of course,* she thought. *At last. Something I can do. Some way to help.*

As soon as Flo got back to their farm in Pennsylvania, she gathered her family around her kitchen table. (It's not a working farm, mind you, but there were 32 animals out in the barn just to keep things interesting.) There was Leonard; her daughters, Margie and Gloria; and her husband, Jim, who at the time worked as a heavy-duty construction surveyor. She told them what she'd seen. She told them how she wanted to make some kind of blanket, quilt, or sleeping bag to make a difference in the ways she could.

"I wasn't out to cure homelessness," she says now of her impulse to help. "I don't know that the problem will ever go away. But people are cold, and I thought I could help keep someone alive tonight so that they might find someone else to help them or heal them tomorrow. That's all it was at first. It was a small thing, but it was a *big* small thing."

With her family, Flo fashioned a primitive homemade sleeping bag from old sheets and blankets. She used worn socks, torn T-shirts, or discarded drapes as filler, for warmth. And when they were done with the first one, they made another. All told, they made eight sleeping bags that first year, and Flo and Jim drove into New York City with the first batch to put them to use.

"You can see the homeless every day," Flo says, "everywhere you look, in a city like New York. There's no avoiding them. Except of course when you want to find someone to help. We drove around for hours, it seemed, just looking for someone who could use one of our sleeping bags, but it was an awful weather day, and we couldn't find anyone. They were probably down in the subways or in abandoned buildings—it was that kind of day. Finally, we were about to give up. We were about to drive over the bridge, back out to Queens, and as we were heading up the on-ramp, I saw a flicker of light in the crack of the wall where the bridge met the pavement. I knew right away it was a cigarette ember, and that someone was taking shelter in that small crawlspace by the bridge, so I had Jim pull over, right there on that on-ramp. There was no traffic, so we just pulled over, and Jim walked over to the wall and said into the night, 'Hey, buddy, can you use a sleeping bag?' An arm came out and took it, and that was the very first bag we gave out."

Now, about 100,000 bags later, Flo Wheatley runs one of the largest homespun, grassroots, backyard social action projects I've ever encountered. Actually, she doesn't so much run it as she does hold on for dear life, because this effort she started keeps getting bigger and bigger every year. Her family distributed 49 bags that second year, and over 400 the following year, and soon enough, their friends and neighbors started to spark to the same notion.

"We didn't have any idea that people knew what we were up to," Flo recalls, "but more and more, people would come by, asking us to teach them what we were doing. Or, they'd drop off some old clothes, some small pieces of material. We live in a town of only 300 people, and in the past year alone, our neighbors dropped off more than 6,000 sleeping bags, all of them fashioned from clean, recycled textiles that people no longer needed. And it all started from that very first bag. So, clearly, it's taken off."

Yes, it certainly has, and Jim Wheatley saw it coming. "He sat us down one night and warned me," Flo remembers." He said, 'Once this leaves our kitchen table, everybody's gonna want in. There'll be no end to it.' And he was right. It's taken over our lives. We're both working it pretty much full-time now that he's retired."

What full-time means is this: Flo and Jim have converted three parking spaces in their four-car garage into a storage facility for the endless supplies of recycled materials that now find them every day. (The other space is used as an office for Flo's home-care business, and the joke on the Wheatley farm is that none of their cars has ever spent a night under a roof.) When she's not checking on FedEx or UPS deliveries; or promoting her project to church, school, and youth groups around the country; or talking to shelters in need of bedding; or recruiting and training new members to her quilting group, Flo finds the time to do "pre-fills" on a table she's got set up on her porch. These she stuffs with all the clean clothes nobody wants from area rummage sales— blankets, sheets, sweaters, and skirts. It used to be that she'd scour the community herself for these items, but now they find her. "I always tell people not to die in Hop Bottom," Flo jokes, "because we even want your underwear."

Folks hear what Flo's up to, and the stuff keeps on coming. Donations of materials. A van, gifted by area churches, to replace the family Volkswagen as the delivery vehicle. Checks, large and small, to pay for gas and shipping. Mostly, though, it's the recycled household textiles that are taking over her home. Really, there's more than she can use, and other members of her ever-growing grassroots organization, My Brothers' Keeper Quilt Group, come and go as they please, in and out of the Wheatley garage, taking supplies, leaving supplies. The door's always open, Flo says, and as of this writing, her mailing list of friends and volunteers has grown to 10,000—and every last one of them has had a hand in crafting at least one sleeping bag.

Most of My Brothers' Keeper's bags come out looking the same, save for the differences in the original fabric, and the weight and heft of the fill. The sleeping bag is made by cutting scrap material, bedspreads, drapes, or rummage into the largest square or rectangle the piece will allow. Next, these pieces are sewn into two 7' x 7' squares, which are used to form the sleeping bag cover, top and bottom. The cover is then filled with old blankets, mattress pads, socks, under-wear, fiberfill . . . whatever the quilters can get their hands on. This, in turn, is sandwiched into place by the companion 7' x 7' cover. The bag is then rolled and tied with straps, often discarded neckwear. Flo's group suggests that quilters include a few personal items inside the bedroll: clean underwear, socks, hat, a scarf, a toothbrush. She also encourages adding a nonjudgmental message of hope; or words of an appropriate hymn, poem, or prayer.

"It's an imperfect project," Flo admits, "but that's the whole idea. That's why we call them

'Ugly Quilts.' These bags aren't meant to last a lifetime. Some of them don't last a month. The point is that they shouldn't be so well done that you can't part with them once you've finished. And if it should get dirty or wet or thrown away the day after you've made it, you're not gonna cry. Even if it's just used for one night, it's made a big difference in someone's life. Every year, we start with sleeping bag number one. The idea is that once it's destroyed, you're cold again, and if you need a second one—if you're cold again—we're going to make one for you. If we took too long on each bag, if we fussed over every last detail, we'd never get the kind of production we need to meet the demand."

That demand varies depending on the season. If a shelter calls and expresses a need, Flo and her group rise to meet it. In the winter, they turn out about 500 bags each week in Hop Bottom alone. Production also varies. Six sets of practiced hands, working together around a proper table can produce a sleeping bag in about 20 minutes, from start to finish. (Of course, these times can vary—one church ran a sew-off, pitting mothers against daughters, and the younger generation managed to start and finish a bag in less than 15 minutes!)

As word of Flo's initiative has spread, those six sets of hands are getting together all across the country—in church basements, on kitchen tables, in high schools and middle schools. This year, the Girl Scouts of America have added the My Brothers' Keeper's Sleeping Bag effort to its list of recognized community service projects. High school home economics teachers seem to love the project for the way it accommodates imperfection; even a poorly made bag offers welcome relief on a cold night. There's even a maximum-security women's prison in Connecticut where the project has been embraced as a way for inmates to remain connected to the outside world—to feel useful and productive, and to remain human in an inhumane setting.

"The leader of that quilting group has been in jail for 14 years, and she's got another 30 to go," Flo explains, "and yet she's taken to this like it's a lifeline. Can you imagine? In a maximum-security prison? The warden says if one needle goes missing, the group shuts down, but they've been together now for three years. We went up to visit them when they completed their 100th sleeping bag, and almost every one of these women told me that if they'd received this kind of help when they were out on the streets, maybe their lives would have turned out differently."

About the only place the idea hasn't hit has been in our inner cities, and Flo has a theory on this. "If someone is peeing on your doorstep, you're not going to have too much sympathy for them," she reasons. Indeed, My Brothers' Keeper has even fielded its share of criticism from community action groups who charge that this kind of project enables drug addiction and helplessness, and perpetuates homelessness, but whenever Flo hears this kind of talk, she turns the other cheek.

"If people choose not to participate in what we're doing, that's fine," she says. "There are enough people who see the good in it that we're able to make a difference. We're not out to solve this huge social problem. We're out to help each other, one person at a time. To make each night more tolerable. To keep someone alive until he or she is able to find it in themselves to seek help or healing. When I think of the homeless, I ask myself, 'What would Christ do?' And the answer always comes back the same: He would reach out, same as we're doing."

It's been years since Flo has kept an accurate count of the total number of sleeping bags that have come from that one kindness, but she and the My Brothers' Keeper's board of directors work to measure the tonnage that comes and goes from the farm. They have weekly mail meetings to ensure that every donation receives a personal thank-you note, and there's always a piece of paperwork to be filed to meet various not-for-profit requirements. There are also a number of state-backed programs that need to be tracked, to ensure that the group's efforts have maximum impact on the community. There's now an in-kind grant in Pennsylvania, for example, that allows a home county to provide shelter to a homeless family when a certain number of sleeping bags have been donated within that county.

Has it gotten to the point where Flo herself is no longer surprised by the abundant generosity of people? "I'm surprised every day," she says. "And do you know why? It's because we don't claim to own this project. It's just an idea. It may have started with us, but it doesn't end with us. If someone wants to grab on to it, they can. On their own time, in their own way. There are no rules. Just do as much as you can with what you have. Do what your community needs. Once you've satisfied the need in your own area, you can reach out through the United Way referral service to the next community in need, and so on.

"All of it is done on a volunteer basis," Flo says of the grassroots effort. "All of our materials are recycled or donated. Even the deliveries are made depending on where you travel. If someone in our group is going to Philadelphia, she'll call in and tell us she can take so many bags. I'll give them an address of a shelter that could use them, and off they'll go. If there's no shelter waiting, we hand them out ourselves. This, I think, is the reason people have taken to this project in such a big way. They take it in the way that they live, contributing what they can, when they can. Take it in the path that you travel, that's our rule, and all in a cost-free way. It makes a difference in so many ways. In the lives of the homeless individuals on the receiving end of our work. In *our* own lives, which have been enriched by the project, and the new friendships that have come from it. And even in our environment. After almost 20 years, we haven't even made a dent in people's attics, closets, and garages. There's all this wonderful, clean, usable material out there, trapped in people's homes. When you think about it, it's one of our great untapped resources, and we might as well mine it."

From time to time, Flo finds herself thinking of that homeless man who escorted her and her ailing son out to Queens. Her angel. She can still picture him, with his glassless frames, leaning in that taxicab window, imploring her not to forget him, and she draws pride and comfort in knowing that she hasn't. *Don't abandon me*. She's never lost those words, and she guesses she never will. She's never seen that homeless man again— wouldn't that have been something?—to let him know what his kindness has wrought, but she likes to think he knows. Somehow. She likes to think that one of her bags has made its way to him. Somehow.

My Brothers' Keeper volunteers don't hear much from any of the recipients of their handiwork, but there was one time, at a crafts show in an armory in Wilkes-Barre, Pennsylvania, when Flo could feel it in the air and in her bones that their efforts had been appreciated. She was handing out flyers, trying to recruit additional quilters and maybe raise some awareness, when she noticed a man looking at her from across the large room. She tried not to stare back so as not to embarrass him, but he was there in the corner of her eye for the longest time. After a while, he walked over to her and placed a five-dollar bill on the display table she'd set up. She wasn't selling anything, wasn't asking for money, but the man set down the bill as if she had it coming. And Flo could just tell. She could feel it. She knew this man must have received one of their bags, back during a rough patch, and was only now realizing where it had come from. She may have been off in her assessment, but I don't think it matters, because in that one moment, she was able to draw a line from where she'd been on that miserable Monday afternoon on Lexington Avenue with her son, Leonard, to where she was now, working tirelessly to make a difference—not to change the world necessarily, but to make it a little more comfortable.

✳ ✳ ✳

Donations of recycled textiles fill the Wheatleys' garage.

More than 100,000 "My Brothers' Keeper's" quilts have been distributed worldwide.

"Even if it's used for just one night, it's made a difference in someone's life."

*Denny stretches out before
the race begins.*

CHAPTER TWELVE

No Excuses

Every time I can't get going in the morning, every time I ache and sweat and shake, every time I think about cutting my workouts short for no good reason, I think of this guy, Dennis Chipollini, a United Parcel Service (UPS) worker from outside Philadelphia. And when I do, I know I'm not alone.

You see, Denny moves about as not-so-quiet inspiration to anyone who's ever confronted a crippling injury or chronic illness. I choose those words carefully, *not-so-quiet*, because this is someone who makes a lot of noise and calls attention to his efforts. He doesn't do his thing in a vacuum, and that's precisely his point. After all, he figures, where's the profit in beating the odds, confounding medical experts, and pushing himself to extremes if there's no one to notice? If there's no one to think, *Hey, if this guy can do what he's doing, then I can do anything.*

There's a lot to notice about Denny Chipollini. For one thing, he's always moving. For another, he's got this infectious enthusiasm for whatever it is that's got his attention, or whatever goal he's placed in his sights. It's not until later that you notice the prosthetic device where his left leg used to be, the relentless drive in place of his old complacency, or the rock-hard abs and stomach muscles that don't seem to fit in with the rest of his picture.

Denny wasn't always this way, and he wants people to know that about him. It took a disabling car accident and a devastating diagnosis for his son to get Denny pointed in the right direction. I'll take the car accident first. It was September 16, 1989, a Saturday morning, and Denny was off to his parents' place for breakfast in the middle of a hard rain. His wife, Susan, was seven months pregnant with their first child, and she wasn't up for the outing. Denny had gone about three miles on the New Jersey Turnpike when his 1986 black Thunderbird started to hydroplane. It happened in an instant. The car turned sideways. The brakes didn't respond. Denny braced for impact, and the car careened into a metal guardrail by the side of the road.

"There was all this dust and smoke when I hit," Denny recalls, "and when everything cleared, I thought I was okay. Looking back, that's one of the weirdest parts of it. I thought to myself, *Ooooh, all right, that was a close one.* I really felt like I was okay. I touched my arms, my chest, my face. Everything seemed fine. Then I looked down."

What he saw was pretty frightening. When the car careened, the guardrail managed to splice the front of the car, virtually cutting off Denny's legs like a guillotine. The rail hadn't been capped, or run into the ground, and its jagged edge was somehow able to knife through the wheel well at precisely the wrong angle. Denny's left leg was on top of the dashboard, visibly broken to where the bone was piercing through the skin; his right leg was pinned under the rail on the passenger side, and it seemed to Denny to be attached to the rest of him by a single artery, stretched like a rubber band and a small strip of skin.

"When I saw that, my heart just raced," he tells. "Blood came out of that thing like a super-soaker, and with the realization came the pain. This great rush of pain. And then panic. I thought to myself, *Okay, you've got to calm down or you're going to die.* I was having agonizing pain, but I quickly realized I had to slow my heart down some or it would be over for me—I'd bleed to death right there, so I tried to visualize myself hours ahead of where I was at the time, in some emergency room somewhere, doctors working on me, with everything turning out okay. That's what I told myself, that everything was gonna be okay, and I kinda raced forward in my thinking to where the worst was over. When I did that, the blood flow slowed. My heartbeat slowed. I started to get a little comfortable. I was still in a lot of pain, but it eased some. It became manageable."

The trouble was, Denny's visualization technique didn't account for the condition of his car on the side of the road. As bad as it was, it didn't *look* all that bad. If you didn't happen to witness the accident as it happened, you'd never have never figured it out for the aftermath; the car, at rest, just looked like it was parked sideways on the turnpike. You couldn't really see the guardrail piercing through the cab on a passing glance, so for the longest time, nobody stopped to offer help. The accident was bad enough, the condition of Denny's legs were bad enough, and yet on top of that, he had to deal with the worry that no one would think to offer help. The driver's-side window had been cracked the tiniest bit because of the rain, but the power had been cut in the crash, and all Denny could do was stick his fingers out in a desperate distress call. There wasn't a thing he could do to get anyone's attention, short of crawling out of the car himself, and that wasn't about to happen, not the way the guardrail had him pinned in.

"It was at this point," he says, "that I started to make my deals with God. I thought about the baby. I prayed, *Lord, please, let me live to see the birth of my child.* I went from trying to calm down, to slow the blood flow, to getting nervous again over the fact that no one was stopping. It felt like 20 minutes. Maybe it was 10 or 15, but it felt longer. Finally, someone came."

A turnpike crew worker happened by and helped Denny fashion a tourniquet from an old rag and the Thunderbird's turn signal lever, and when the guy twisted the thing, Denny ripped the steering wheel off the column, that's how much pain he was in. The crewman had already radioed in for help, but neither one of them thought they should wait for the medics, so they went ahead with their desperate measures.

Denny's not the sort of guy to sit back and wait for someone else to do for him what he's quite capable of doing for himself, and this right here was a good example. When medical attention finally did arrive, the talk right away was to amputate what was left of Denny's right leg, right on the spot. There was no saving it, the EMT guys said. Denny was already shot through with painkillers, but he could make out what they were saying just outside the cab of the car. He pleaded with the medics not to take his leg, to give him some time, and eventually they used the Jaws of Life to separate the guardrail from his foot and managed to cut the roof back to lift him out. It was raining fairly steady, and the turnpike would be shut down for two hours, and back home, Denny's parents were starting to worry because he hadn't shown up for breakfast yet. Once his wife, Susan, was called to see what time he'd left, she started to think in worst-case scenarios, too. Sometime later, when Susan heard that the turnpike was shut down due to an accident, she knew in her bones that Denny was involved.

Eventually, Denny's mind-body visualization technique landed him in the emergency room, just as he knew it would, but there was no way he could have anticipated the ordeal that lay waiting. The screws and rods and pins that would have to be attached to his legs. The external fixators. The major operations. The infections. Fifteen operations in all, ending with the amputation of his left leg below the knee. Ironically, at the accident scene, he had to talk the medics out of cutting off his right leg, and what finally happened was that he had to beg his doctors to take his left.

At this point, he was a couple months into his rehabilitation and recovery, and there was one problem after another with his left leg. He was in tremendous pain, facing a lifetime of inactivity. His doctors were telling him he'd never walk again, but Denny wasn't buying it. He had his father bring in his free weights from home, and he started working the dumbbells from his bed. He even adjusted the bedframe to where his legs were up as far as they'd go, and he started doing sit-ups until they burned. And when they did, he did 20 more. Denny's doctors were super aggressive about keeping the leg—at one point, his white blood count was so low visitors had to wear a mask—but the prognosis was grim.

And the grimmer it got, the more determined Denny became. To beat back whatever ordeal he was facing. To reclaim his life. To defy the long odds against him.

"Everyone was real anxious about me not losing my leg," he explains, "but I couldn't see an end to this ordeal, and at one point, I got a call from a family friend trying to convince me not to go through with the amputation. He'd been in a similar accident, and his leg was in a similar situation, and family members had been on him to give me a call, to show me that life would go on after everything had a chance to heal. So I asked the guy, 'What do you do all day?' And he explained how he couldn't do much of anything, how he got around on crutches, how he sat in front of his window and watched the neighborhood kids play in the park. 'But I still have my leg,' he said, and I thought, *What good is it?* This guy was supposed to call to show me how lucky he was, that he still had his leg, but he couldn't run, couldn't walk, couldn't get around. He was still in constant pain. I hung up the phone feeling better about an amputation. I knew this was what it would take to start my life again. I wanted to get rid of this infected part of me. I knew there was technology out there to help me move, to get me active, so the call kinda had the opposite effect, but I was real happy with it. My doctors told me later they'd never seen someone go into an operation like this with a smile on their face, but I was smiling."

Somewhere in the middle of all this, Denny's son, Nicholas, made his appearance. It was the strangest thing, Denny on one floor of the hospital, being prepped for one of his major surgeries, and Susan giving birth on another nurses, family, and friends running back and forth with bulletins. They hadn't known it would be a boy, but Denny was thrilled. He would have been thrilled either way, but mostly he was thrilled to have made it to this moment. He was actually coming out of surgery when Nicholas was born, and a couple of nurses brought the baby into the recovery room. Denny was kind of out of it, coming to after the anesthesia, and he remembers seeing a little angel with wings. He thought, *Whoa, what am I seeing?* He put together that this was his son, who looked like a little doll with a tiny hat on his head to keep in the warmth, and this part made perfect sense, but then there was the piece about the wings. He thought he was hallucinating. Of course, sometime later, he learned that the hospital staff slapped a pair of these little angel wings on all the newborns, but at the time, it was a trip.

Back home, right in the middle of the hard road he was facing, Denny did what he could to get past his new circumstance. For a while in there, he wasn't able to do much. He couldn't put his legs below his waist for the circulation, so he had to move about in a strange crawl, on his butt. He couldn't go back to his job at UPS anytime soon, and a part of him worried that he'd never go back at all. His mother came by five days a week to help look after the baby and Denny. His wife had to go back to work. Poor Susan never even got a chance to experience the joys of first-time motherhood. To call the Chipollini's financial situation bleak would have been to put a positive spin on it. They were down to the last $100 in their checking account. There was no time for Hallmark sentiments or Kodak moments.

"I didn't realize it at the time," he assesses, "but all of this took a toll on our marriage. Susan got cheated out of motherhood. There was all this doting on me, everyone worrying how I was gonna get around, and would I be okay. People coming to visit me. I didn't see it, but everything was all about me, and that was a huge problem. We had a new mother in the house, a brand-new child, and there I was with my constant worries. *Where am I going? Do I have a job? Will I ever walk again?* It wasn't at all like we'd planned."

Just then, just when it seemed like things couldn't get any bleaker, Denny's world took a positive turn, and he and Susan found themselves facing down the biggest sentimental moment in the history of sentimental moments. A group of family and friends got together to organize a benefit to help the Chipollinis with their bills and with Nicholas. The generosity and affection stormed them by surprise and blew them away. People didn't just contribute money— they gave their time, their love, and their energy. They shopped for groceries. They baby-sat for Nicholas. They helped around the house. Basically, they filled in the cracks so that Susan and Denny could get their lives going again. It was a wonderful thing to see, and it attracted the kind of neighborhood, word-of-mouth attention that made the local newspaper pick up on it.

Soon, people Denny didn't even know were sending money. At night, after he'd struggled into bed, his mother would bring up stacks and stacks of mail, and Denny would go through it in disbelief. The outpouring of love and generosity was overwhelming. All told, folks kicked in over $30,000—checks, cash, small change—which took a huge bite out of their medical bills and bridged some of the gap in what Denny had been earning. They were still scraping by, but this first miracle bought them some time to go looking for another.

It also lit a fire under Denny and got him thinking that he was going to work like a dog to get himself stronger, and moving—show folks he might have been *down*, but he wasn't *out*. That would be how he could repay these good people, to show them that their kindness was the push he needed to make himself whole. He started rolling his own wheelchair ten miles each day through his neighborhood, building up his upper body, getting out in the world, circulating. The exercise itself was a positive, but it was also a kind of therapy—a mental and spiritual lift. Soon enough, he was moving about on crutches. The doctors told him to bear weight on his residual limb for a few minutes each day, which would also strengthen his left leg, which had never fully healed, and Denny took these as marching orders. He started walking two miles a day, figuring if a couple minutes was good for him, then a couple miles would be even better. He didn't tell his doctors for fear they would talk him down from this approach. He just went at it in his own way. The pain, he says now, was excruciating, but he kept at it. He refused to sit still and accept his fate— but found himself constantly pushing the pain barrier, attacking everything, full tilt, all the time.

Ten months after the accident, Denny was walking with a cane, and on the anniversary of the crash, he took his stickshift car out for a drive. He never left the development, but still. Life had become a series of challenges to be met and mastered, and Denny had set it up in his head as this great big deal, to be able to drive his car again within a year of the accident, and there he was, driving. Within two years, he was back on the job at UPS—not quite the same job, mind you, but he was working. Behind a desk (sort of), doing quality control, tracking receipts, that sort of thing. The folks at work had kind of written him off after the accident, but here he was, back at it. The same job, but different.

And he wasn't done yet. Less than four years after the accident, Denny set his sights on a local five-kilometer race, thinking it was something he could do—and that, in the doing, he might learn something about the new spirit he'd been harnessing, see what kind of paces he could put his body through. He did most of his training on a bicycle, mixed with some running when his leg was up for it, and he managed to call on reserves of will and drive and finish the race. He came in dead last, but he finished, and when it was over, a little boy came over to Denny and redirected his life. "Mister," the kid said, "you're my hero."

"It just floored me," Denny says now, of this post-race encounter. "A little kid, maybe eight or nine years old. I felt this incredible rush. Pride, energy, purpose . . . I didn't know what it was, or what I'd do with it, but I realized I'd stumbled onto something that could help people. This was a fully able-bodied kid, completely healthy as far as I could tell, but I started to imagine the kind of impact I could have on someone who was disabled."

As it turned out, this was one of those realizations you don't quite know what to do with at the time, and it took Denny a couple years to crystallize his thinking and move forward in a systematic way. During that time, though, he had to face another curveball—this one, a devastating piece of news about his son, Nicholas. This was the upsetting diagnosis I hinted at earlier. For a couple of years, Nicholas had been having problems focusing on certain tasks. His mind would wander, or he'd appear to drift off in thought. The problem first surfaced in day care, as Nicholas first began to interact with other children in a structured environment, and as he moved through preschool and on into kindergarten, it became more apparent. At first, doctors thought it was Attention Deficit Disorder (ADD), which these days seems to be affecting more and more of our children. Then, it was thought that Nicholas might be suffering from Asperger's Syndrome, a form of autism, and for another while, they believed his problems were heart related.

In the end, they came back with a frightening diagnosis: neurofibromatosis, or NF, a genetic disorder that can lead to vision and behavioral problems. Denny and Susan had never heard of NF; no one they knew had ever heard of it either, but they made themselves a quick study. The most visible aspect of NF, they learned, was the aggressive freckling and café-au-lait marks all over the body. The most dangerous aspect was the thousands of tiny tumors that tended to form in nerve-rich areas, such as the eyes, the brain, and the spinal cord. These tumors could grow inside the body, or outside, and Nicholas would have to be constantly monitored. There is no known cure.

"We met patients covered with these tumors from head to toe," Denny reveals. "The tumors can turn malignant. Remove them and they'll grow back, sometimes in clusters. In a milder case, you might never see a tumor. In 60 percent of NF cases, you also see some form of ADD, or other learning disabilities. In Nicholas's case, he also had Tourette's Syndrome, so as he got older, school really started becoming a problem for him. Two years ago, he had a horrible year. He was ten years old, in the fourth grade, and his self-esteem was in the toilet. You know how cruel kids can be at that age. They called him names. He ate lunch by himself. He had no friends. He played team sports, but his own teammates would tease him. He'd come home after school and go straight to his room and get lost in a fantasy world."

It was somewhere during these struggles to get Nicholas a proper diagnosis and a plan of attack for the hard road ahead that Denny thought back to that small boy he had met on the course of that 5K race. *You're my hero*. The words fairly echoed in his head and gave him an idea. Maybe there was some way to harness the kind of attention he received in that small local race, and use it to call positive attention to NF and other childhood diseases. And, perhaps, in the calling of that attention, he could also erase some of the social stigma attached to illnesses like NF, to take a bite out of some of the teasing in school, to get kids to look on each other with a little more compassion.

With this in mind, Denny entered the Philadelphia Distance Run, a half-marathon that in 1999 happened to be held on the tenth anniversary of the car crash, almost to the day. Denny had these goals: to finish, but to not finish last, and to increase awareness of NF. He wasn't out to raise money so much as the collective consciousness. He held out the race as a way to thank his family and friends for their extra efforts, and as a rallying point for anyone facing a difficult path. It wasn't every day that a man looked to run a half-marathon on a prosthetic leg, so when the newspapers came calling, Denny made sure to make his case. He spoke out about the need for NF research, and he shone a light on some of the particular ways kids with NF are made to struggle. They live with tremendous uncertainty, never knowing where the disease might take them, and they're too often ostracized by their peers. He wanted to get a dialogue going, and he found his soapbox in the press interviews he gave before and after the race. Every local television station, every local radio station, every local newspaper . . . everyone wanted to talk to this guy running the race on one leg—the guy who'd been told by his doctors he'd never walk again. And all this guy wanted to talk about were the brave kids he'd met at Philadelphia Children's Hospital, the stories of hope and courage he'd collected in the short time since Nicholas had been diagnosed.

Once again, Denny finished the race, this time deep in the middle of the pack, and Nicholas and his little sister, Elyse, joined their father for the home stretch and crossed the finish line as a family. Talk about your Kodak moments.

Since then, Denny's gone on to complete full marathons in San Diego and Pittsburgh. Next up: Chicago, New York, Los Angeles, and Boston. Each time out, he shaves a little bit off his time, learns a little bit more what his body and his residual limb and his prosthetic device are capable of, and pushes himself a little bit more. And each time out, he delivers the message that has underpinned his life since his accident: "No excuses, no limits."

"I've learned so much from what's happened to me," he reflects, "and from what Nicholas is going through. I learned that if you don't take action, nothing's gonna happen. It's basic. Through positive action, I've had so much positive reaction. It's not just my rehabilitation. It's not just how Nicholas has taken a bad situation at school and worked to turn it around. It's how we can all turn a corner in our lives and move forward. When I talk to school groups, I tell kids that there are three things they need to do in life. The first is to find out who they really are, to look past the glitter and the gold and the status and find their true, inner selves. The second, once they find that person, is to challenge it, and to continue to challenge it. Life is not meant to be comfortable or easy. When life gets too easy, no action is taken, and you might as well throw the dirt on right then. We labor under this false industrial philosophy. We work hard for 30 years, give the best years of our lives to a job or a career, and the goal is to retire and enjoy a life of leisure. What kind of goal is that? Where's the challenge in that? It's idiotic. You work all your life to do nothing? You might as well die. So, yeah, challenge yourself constantly. Push yourself. Try something new. Set new goals. I'm not saying you have to reach every goal you set, but if you can't make it to one, break off and go after another one. Keep reaching.

"The third thing I tell kids is to take somebody with them. It's not enough to challenge yourself. You've got to reach out and bring someone along for the ride. Push the guy next to you. Lend a hand. Help someone else. You do yourself an injustice if you don't. You sell yourself short. I know, because that's how it was with me. I was never a charitable person. I was pretty self-absorbed before my accident. I was a good person, but I didn't do much for other people. But now that I'm out there, motivating others, setting an example, pushing myself to physical extremes, I feel whole."

The great thing about Denny Chipollini is that nothing's enough. He started out running five kilometers to make his point, then he moved on to a half-marathon (13.1 miles), and from there to a full marathon (26.2 miles). His latest plan is to travel the entire country on foot, coast to coast. He's going to spread his No Excuses message along the way, spotlighting NF and other childhood diseases, and celebrating the wonderful mix of guts and inspiration and desire that rests within us all.

❀ ❀ ❀

The challenge begins.

Denny running closer to the finish line.

A sigh of relief after completing 26.2 miles.

Denny receives a warm embrace after crossing the finish line.

Appendix

*F*or more information on **The Bald Eagles Foundation,** a nonprofit youth-based cancer support network, please contact: Shawn O'Gorman at (760) 598-8897.

To find out more about **Eddie Lama and the Oasis Animal Sanctuary**, please contact: Faunavision, c/o Eddie Lama, 163 Third Ave., Suite 320, New York, NY 10003 • (212) 459-4825 **www.oasissanctuary.org.**

For more information about **Camp Aldersgate/Med Camps,** please contact: Camp Aldersgate, Inc., c/o Sarah Spencer, 2000 Aldersgate Rd., Little Rock, AR 72205.

For more information on **Irving Roth** and on becoming a supporter of the **Holocaust Resource Center,** please contact: Irving Roth, 333 Searingtown Rd., Manhasset, NY 11030.

For more information on **Sulieman Beyah,** please contact: Smiling Hands, Inc., c/o Sulieman Beyah, 5409 Euclid St., Philadelphia, PA 19131.

For more information on **Flo Wheatley's Sleeping Bag Project,** please contact: My Brothers' Keeper Quilt Group, Strawberry Hill Farm, R.R.1, Box 1049, Hop Bottom, PA 18824 **www.uglyquilts.org.**

For additional information on **Denny Chipollini,** please contact him at: Generation Hope, P.O. Box 1392, Skippack, PA 19474 • **dennychipollini@netscape.net.**

❀ ❀ ❀

About the Author

*M*ontel *Williams* is the Emmy Award-winning host of the nationally syndicated *Montel* show. As a highly decorated former Naval intelligence officer, motivational speaker, actor, and humanitarian, Williams is an example of personal achievement for people throughout the country. He is the author of *Mountain, Get Out of My Way* and *Life Lessons and Reflections;* the co-author of *Practical Parenting* and *BodyChange;* and the proud father of four children.

❋ ❋ ❋

✸ ✸ ✸

We hope you enjoyed
this Mountain Movers Press/Hay House book.
If you would like to receive additional information,
please contact:

MOUNTAIN

MOVERS
PRESS

c/o Hay House, Inc.
P. O. Box 5100
Carlsbad, CA 92018-5100

(760) 431-7695 or **(800) 654-5126**
(760) 431-6948 (fax) or **(800) 650-5115 (fax)**

Please visit the Hay House Website at: **hayhouse.com**

✸ ✸ ✸